SPIRITUAL DIRECTION

A Guide to Giving & Receiving Direction

GORDON T. SMITH

IVP Books
An imprint of InterVarsity Press
Downers Grove, Illinois

InterVarsity Press
P.O. Box 1400, Downers Grove, IL 60515-1426
World Wide Web: www.ivpress.com
Email: email@ivpress.com

InterVarsity Press® *is the book-publishing division of InterVarsity Christian Fellowship/USA*®, *a movement of students and faculty active on campus at hundreds of universities, colleges and schools of nursing in the United States of America, and a member movement of the International Fellowship of Evangelical Students. For information about local and regional activities, write Public Relations Dept., InterVarsity Christian Fellowship/USA, 6400 Schroeder Rd., P.O. Box 7895, Madison, WI 53707-7895, or visit the IVCF website at www.intervarsity.org.*

Scripture quotations, unless otherwise noted, are from the New Revised Standard Version of the Bible, *copyright 1989 by the Division of Christian Education of the National Council of the Churches of Christ in the USA. Used by permission. All rights reserved.*

While all stories in this book are true, some names and identifying information in this book have been changed to protect the privacy of the individuals involved.

Cover design: Cindy Kiple
Interior design: Beth Hagenberg
Images: Leaf illustration © *mxtama/iStockphoto*
        Two birds in a tree © *Amy Weiss /Trevillion Images*

ISBN 978-0-8308-3579-9 (print)
ISBN 978-0-8308-6470-6 (digital)

Printed in the United States of America ∞

Library of Congress Cataloging-in-Publication Data

A catalog record for this book is available from the Library of Congress.

P	17	16	15	14	13	12	11	10	9	8	7	6	5	4	3	2	1
Y	28	27	26	25	24	23	22	21	20	19	18	17	16	15	14		

to joella

Contents

1 The Ministry of Spiritual Direction.   9

2 Theological Perspectives   19

3 Focused Conversation   39

4 Attending to What Is Happening in Our Prayers   51

5 A Spiritual Direction Session   59

6 Pastoral Ministry, Evangelism and Friendship   69

7 The Qualities and Character of a Director   81

8 The Qualities and Character of a Directee   89

9 The Holy Spirit as Spiritual Director   93

Notes   97

For Further Reading   99

1

The Ministry of
Spiritual Direction

We are not alone—or, better put, we do not need to be alone and we are not meant to be alone, particularly when it comes to our attempts to make sense of God's presence in our lives.

We each need to take personal responsibility for our own growth in faith, hope and love. A maturing Christian will desire to push deeper into studying Scripture and not expect to be spoon-fed Bible teaching. Likewise, each of us is called into a mature adult faith in Christ. We grow in confidence as we discern and make the key decisions that guide our lives.

And yet, while we each live the Christian life to which we are personally and individually called, we are not alone in this journey. We are part of the faith community; we have the joy of knowing others on the road who support us, encourage us, teach us, guide us and provide correction as necessary. Indeed, as we grow into an adult faith we learn, at each stage of the way, that we cannot make it on our own.

There is a certain irony here: the more mature we are in our faith, the more we recognize our need for others—companions, friends, pastors and spiritual directors. Each of these is a gift from God, a means by which we might appropriate God's grace and respond to God's call on our lives. Potentially, one of the more significant of these gifts is the ministry of *spiritual direction*.

THE MINISTRY OF SPIRITUAL DIRECTION

A *spiritual director* offers spiritual guidance and companionship to help us make sense of our faith journey, interpret with us the significant markers on the road, and encourage us, particularly through the more difficult transitions and valleys of our pilgrimage. Most of all, a spiritual director helps us make sense of the witness of the Spirit—assisting us to respond well to the question, How is God present to me and how is God, through the ministry of the Spirit, at work in my life?

Even if we have been Christians and maturing in our faith for many years, we still need the encouragement and guidance that might come through spiritual direction. Only pride would lead us to think we could go it alone. Genuine humility is evident in our realization that we need a companion, a fellow pilgrim and Christian, who can help us discern and foster an attentiveness to God's presence in our lives. This is the gift of spiritual direction.

Some might prefer that we use a different designation to describe this ministry. They suggest that the term *director* seems too authoritative or invasive, that the language of direction implies more actual direction than is appropriate—for only Christ is Lord and thus only Christ should actually direct. Many suggest that spiritual mentor might be a better designation, or perhaps spiritual companion or spiritual friend. As Simon

Chan notes, there are some who resist the implied authority in the term *director* and prefer something more obviously egalitarian, something that connotes the other as one who comes alongside but does not actually "direct."[1]

I concur with Chan's observation that the language of spiritual friendship suggests another kind of relationship—an equally important one, but a different ministry and relationship. As I will discuss in chapter two, the mentoring relationship is also a different grace in our lives. And while *companion* might be an appropriate way to speak of direction, the issue with each of these alternatives is the resistance to the idea of real authority in the life of the Christian believer.

To some degree, of course, the concern is legitimate. And yet *spiritual direction* is a tested and in a sense ancient designation. Further, all ministries, regardless of their name—be it pastor or apostle or evangelist—are open to abuse and the imposition of one person's will on that of another. Changing a standard label does not remove that potential problem. But more specifically, the language of direction is so very appropriate in the sense that to direct is to be a companion with a very specific agenda: to help the other direct heart and mind to listen to the one most needed, Christ Jesus. We are like Eli who urged—indeed, directed—the young man Samuel to be attentive, to recognize the presence and voice of God and to respond appropriately. William Barry and William Connolly, in *The Practice of Spiritual Direction*, suggest that the language of direction implies that this conversation, in particular, is not casual, aimless or incidentally "along the way," but focused and intentional.[2]

Spiritual direction has a very clear agenda: *directing our attention to the presence of God in our lives*. The language of direction recalls for us the legitimate place of spiritual authority and accountability in our lives. But first and foremost, spiritual direction is the ministry of directing our thoughts and the movements of our hearts toward God and the presence of God in our lives.

A spiritual director urges us to focus our thoughts—to direct our heart and mind—to God. This is typically and rightly done gently and perhaps by way of either question or suggestion. As a rule, we will not feel the force of the director's presence or intentions as much as the gracious nudging, the gentle urging that calls our attention back to God. A director might ask, "Where do you sense the presence of God in your life at this time?" or perhaps offer a suggestion: "As I listen to you, I wonder if it might not be good to consider the following course of action." In either instance, the intent is the same: through question or suggestion this companion is *directing* our attention to the presence of God in our lives.

We need this. Perhaps it is too much to say that the ministry of spiritual direction is indispensable in our lives. And yet, for many of us it is *invaluable*. It is a vital dimension of the way in which pastoral care and formation equip us for our lives and our work, fostering our capacity for prayer and the deepening of our faith. And many are coming to see direction as an essential element of pastoral ministry. Both ordained and lay leaders in the church will find that many members of the congregation would benefit from this ministry if and as it is available.

SPIRITUAL DIRECTION: AN ANCIENT PRACTICE

Spiritual direction is not a new ministry for the church. For many evangelical Christians, the emphasis on spiritual direction seems to be a recent development. But this is an ancient practice, and for many chapters in the history of the church it was an integral part of pastoral ministry. We know of remarkable tales of fourth- and fifth-century Christians heading into the desert to seek the insight and counsel of the desert fathers and mothers. And over the centuries this has been, for many Christians of many different theological and spiritual traditions, a means by which they have found substantive guidance and encouragement. The renewal of this practice for contemporary Christians gives us the opportunity to draw on the wisdom of the church, to learn how it can be most fruitful for us in our current circumstances and, in so doing, to encourage one another in the Christian journey.

What I share in this book is very dependent on this heritage in the church, and certain voices are particularly noteworthy. Most of these are from the Roman Catholic side of the Christian "neighborhood." There is no doubt that the Roman Catholic theological and spiritual heritage has given more attention to spiritual direction over the centuries. Within this tradition, of premiere importance is the work of Ignatius Loyola. Ignatian spirituality finds its anchor piece in the *Spiritual Exercises*, which is essentially a guide to prayer—indeed, a guidebook for a spiritual director who monitors and encourages the prayers of another. Ignatius was the founder of the Society of Jesus, typically called the Jesuits. Until recently, the vast majority of spiritual directors were either Jesuits or were trained by Jesuits. As I draw on this tradition, I am particularly indebted to two authors: Thomas H. Green, SJ, who for many years was the director of spiritual formation at San Jose Seminary in Manila, Philippines; and John English, SJ, former retreat director at Loyola House in Guelph, Ontario, Canada.

Another key and indispensable voice is that of John of the Cross who, like Ignatius Loyola, was a religious leader in sixteenth-century Spain. Ignatius, John of the Cross and Teresa of Ávila, his contemporary, were the three major voices of reform and renewal from within the sixteenth-century church. It is helpful to think of them as the southern Reformers: counterparts to Protestant Reformers Martin Luther and John Calvin, and southern in that they largely ministered in the church of modern-day Spain, southern France and Italy. They remained in and sought renewal for the Church of Rome. In his *Living Flame of Love* John of the Cross gives major attention to the ministry of spiritual direction, and his advice and counsel to contemporary spiritual directors is invaluable.

There are also fine contributions to the practice of spiritual direction from the Catholic Benedictines and Salesians (heirs to St. Francis de Sales), as well as Eastern Orthodox, Anglican and Puritan-Reformed traditions.[3] And yet, while much of this book draws on wisdom from more than one stream in the history of the church, three things bring many of us in this ministry back to the Ignatian tradition as a baseline for guidance. Each of these three is particularly valuable to someone who approaches this ministry as an evangelical Christian. First, we find the clear and defining focus on Christ Jesus. Second is the unique use of the Scriptures, particularly the Gospels, in guiding our prayers. Third, so very noteworthy in Ignatius and the *Spiritual Exercises* is the invaluable instruction on the particular place of the affections—the movements of the heart—for those who seek to respond to God's presence in the world and in their lives.

And yet, each of these streams naturally and obviously builds on the precedent that is set by Scripture. We have, for example, the words of St. Paul offered in correspondence with a younger pastor and leader, Timothy. In many respects, the book of 2 Timothy is a model of spiritual direction—as Paul writes to Timothy in direct response to themes and issues that were clearly particular to Timothy. While in this letter we find wisdom for Christians in each culture and generation, it was originally directed to an individual: Paul, writing to Timothy, in response to the specifics of his life. When we draw on the classics of our spiritual heritage, we simply gain further insight into how we might similarly participate in this invaluable ministry in the life of an individual Christian believer.

A PERSONAL MINISTRY

Paul's ministry to Timothy, in 2 Timothy, is particular. This is the genius of spiritual direction—wisdom and guidance and encouragement for *this* pilgrim who is on the way, seeking to grow in faith, hope and love. In our spiritual journey, we need good teaching and effective preaching. We need to be in the company of others and receive the liturgical leadership of those who preside at worship. But we also find much value in spiritual direction as the counterpart to each of these group ministries. Spiritual direction makes the diverse ministries of the church *personal and individual*. Spiritual direction is the ministry of attention to one person, *this* person, at this time and in this place. While there is a limited place for group direction, generally to speak of spiritual direction is to highlight that this is a one-to-one ministry: one person, present to another, attentive to the work of the Spirit in this person's life, relationships, work and especially prayers.

I stress this individuality without hesitation. Yes, we need group religious activities and exercises. We need to be part of the assembly of God's people, the church, for worship: for the ministry of the Word, as we respond to preaching and teaching, and for the shared participation in the Lord's Supper. Participation in the communal exercise of life in Christ—the activities of the faith community—is indispensable. But the beauty of spiritual direction is precisely that at this time and in this place, one person is being considered—not alone, but in the company of one other, a spiritual director. While they are not alone, it is just one who is the focus of reflection, the one receiving direction. If you are the one receiving direction, you can now, in this time and space, give purposeful, focused attention to the state of your own soul. Without apology. And for the director, the call of the moment is to be present to another, just one other.

Many find value in group spiritual direction. But in these pages I am highlighting the indispensability of a conversation where just one child of God is the focus of attention before God and in the presence of a spiritual "father" or "mother" who comes in the name of Christ to listen. With a group, the network of relationships, while valuable, is immediately more complicated. Indeed, it is challenging enough to listen to one person with the kind of focused attention of which I will be speaking here.

While personal and particular, spiritual direction always assumes an external reference—the triune God, present to us in Christ Jesus, and the witness, guidance and encouragement of the Scriptures. Indeed, in many respects, spiritual direction is nothing but two things—assisting the other to make sense of their experience of Christ, and assisting the other to make application of the Scriptures to their specific circumstances. But it is important to stress that spiritual direction is not *merely* the applying of biblical principles to daily living; rather, its power and impact is that we are making sense, director and directee, of the dynamic and immediate presence of God in our lives.

2

Theological Perspectives

As with all ministries of the church, it is vital that we establish the theological vision or perspective by which we enter into the good work of spiritual direction. Definitions are important of course, but just as crucial is our need to speak *theologically* about this ministry. We will look at four theological themes that inform the ministry of spiritual direction:

- A trinitarian perspective on the character of God and the work of God.
- The nature and character of religious experience.
- The particularity of each person as the basis for emphasis on the individual.
- The church as the people of God and a means of grace to the individual.

THE TRIUNE GOD

First and foremost, a theological vision for spiritual direction will reflect a trinitarian understanding of the work of God in the world and in the life of the individual Christian.

We enter into this ministry recognizing the electing call—the initiative—of God the Father, the Creator. In spiritual direction we are *responding*: God is seeking those who will worship him in spirit and in truth (Jn 4:24), and spiritual direction is purposefully Godward in its orientation. While this is certainly true of other ministries (later in this chapter I will distinguish direction from counseling and mentoring), nowhere as much as in worship leadership and spiritual direction do we appreciate the vertical component of our lives and relationships with others. Spiritual direction fosters this Godward orientation, specifically by way of response to the electing grace of God.

When we speak of the Father—the first person of the Trinity—we speak most fundamentally of the one who is the source of all things, and whose goodness permeates all things. Spiritual direction rests on a critical and fundamental assumption: God is good and fundamentally benevolent toward all that he has made. Thus spiritual direction is a ministry that fosters the capacity to live in awareness of the goodness of God: "For the LORD is good; his steadfast love endures forever, and his faithfulness to all generations" (Ps 100:5). And the only possible response to this goodness? Gratitude. Nothing is so fundamental to the spiritual life as learning to give thanks. Why? Because of this fundamental principle: God is good and benevolent toward all.

From this baseline, we can then consider the *focus* of spiritual direction: the second person of the Trinity, Christ Jesus. I say "focus" quite intentionally. The Christian religious tradition is decidedly trinitarian, but it is also radically focused on Christ. To be a Christian disciple is to be a follower of Jesus. Using an ancient motif, the "grace we seek" in direction is to foster the capacity of the directee to know, love and serve Jesus. Jesus is the Lord and Master; the director has real authority, but it is only offered in the name of Christ, the only One to whom ultimate allegiance is owed. And the director's longing and passion is that those being directed might come grow as disciples of the living and ascended Christ. The directee does not in the end respond to or obey the director, but rather with the encouragement and support of the director he or she comes to a greater capacity to walk in obedience to Christ, as faith in Christ is deepened.

We can gain further perspective from John 15:4, where Jesus invites his disciples into a dynamic relationship with himself using the phrase "Abide in me as I abide in you." The ministry of spiritual direction is clearly in service of this agenda: to foster our capacity to abide in Christ and to know the grace of having Christ abiding in us.

Part of the genius of the *Spiritual Exercises* of Ignatius Loyola is this very focus on Jesus—or, more specifically, on the Jesus story: his birth, life, death and resurrection. In prayer and through the guidance of the Exercises, we are drawn into the Jesus story so that our lives are seen and experienced in light of the scope and breadth of who Jesus is and what he has done.

Then we must speak of the Spirit, the third person of the Trinity. Spiritual direction is intentional conversation—deliberate and purposeful—about one thing in particular: the work of the Spirit. We are not speaking in a generic or general or abstract sense of the work of the Spirit. Rather, through our conversation in spiritual direction we are attentive to the *particular* work of the Spirit in this life, the life of the one who has come for direction.

To be a Christian is to walk in the Spirit and to live in response to the initiative and prompting of the Spirit. It is in and by the Spirit that we recognize the call of the Father and are drawn into union with Christ Jesus. It is by the Spirit that we see and feel our need for realignment with the purposes of God in our lives.

Spiritual direction is a ministry that assumes that we do not live self-constructed lives. We are not on a self-improvement project with a few self-help books to guide us on the way and a spiritual director to help us improve—like a life coach, perhaps, who might help us identify and move into patterns or habits that will foster personal success. However helpful or legitimate all of that might be, when we come to spiritual direction we affirm that the Christian life is lived in radical dependence on the Spirit and through intentional response to the Spirit.

This is most centrally where we see a difference between spiritual direction, counseling and mentoring. In counseling, the agenda is typically a problem or issue of concern we have, often a pathology that needs to be constructively addressed. The focus of attention is a presenting concern, and the relationship continues only as far as there is progress in addressing the particular issue that is undermining our capacity to function in relationships and work. Counseling is then by its very nature a temporary relationship. If the relationship is fruitful and effective, we can look forward to the day when the counselor agrees that we no longer need to come in for counseling.

In mentoring, the focus is the development of capacity or particular understanding: a mentor is more like a coach, fostering our ability in a particular task, perhaps. A mentor will be a teacher, not so much in the context of a classroom, but in the actual craft that we long to master—whether it is learning how to drive a car, to play the piano, to be a public speaker or to write. They will come alongside and coach us in this capacity or craft.

However valuable these other contributions are, the work of spiritual direction has a different focus. A spiritual director is not so much a mentor offering us a skill, but rather a co-listener, attending with us to the particular and immediate agenda of the Spirit in our lives. There is certainly overlap in these three dimensions of ministry; wise spiritual directors are attentive to abiding emotional challenges, and good counselors are often alert to God's work in the life of the client. Similarly, a mentor may well be equipping someone in their capacity for prayer, and a good director is at times something of a teacher. Yet the distinction is important. It is best captured in this: in spiritual direction, the presenting issue is not so much a problem or pathology, or an agenda for teaching and capacity development, but rather, precisely and very deliberately, the *immediate* work of the Spirit in the life of the one who has come for direction.

In spiritual direction, we assume that the Spirit sets the agenda—not a problem or issue that is blocking our functioning, and not our immediate desire to master a capacity or craft. In spiritual direction both director and directee are asking: where is the Spirit present to the directee and calling for growth in faith, hope and love? Some counselors make excellent spiritual directors, but many cannot make the crossover because they consistently default, one might say, to the problem-therapy mode. And some mentors make excellent spiritual directors, but only if they let go of their need to set the agenda, to "teach," to be heard, to manage the process. Both can serve as effective spiritual directors only if they can be attuned to the way the Spirit is setting the agenda for the conversation.

The most crucial and pivotal relationship is that between the directee and God—Father, Son and Spirit. And the spiritual director is at pains to encourage and foster this relationship, to do nothing that distracts from God's agenda in the life of this person at this time and place, to cultivate the capacity of another to mature in faith in God and to respond personally and completely to God. In the end, this is the heart of the matter: not whether the directee is responding to the spiritual director, but if and how they are responding to the triune God. All spiritual direction has this as its purpose, goal and passion. One could easily imagine a spiritual director saying, "I really have only one agenda for you and for this ministry: that you would know God, grow in your capacity to hear God, and mature in your faith and obedience to God and to God's call." While you might say this is the same agenda for a counselor or mentor, the difference in spiritual direction is that the focus of our immediate conversation is what we co-discern, through intentional attentiveness, to be the immediate agenda of the Spirit in the life of the one who has come for direction.

RELIGIOUS EXPERIENCE AND THE AFFECTIONS

The trinitarian vision for spiritual direction is complemented by another vital theological principle and perspective: the nature or character of religious experience, that is, the Christian's experience of God.

We must first recognize that spiritual direction rests on the assumption that each Christian believer has the capacity for an *immediate* relationship with Christ. This means that the Christian, in real time, encounters the crucified, risen and ascended Lord. This was the great passion of Ignatius Loyola in the *Spiritual Exercises*: to foster our capacity, through our prayers, to know Christ, to meet Christ, to hear Christ and to feel the force of that presence—in particular, to feel the love and goodness of his presence. We are not merely talking *about* Christ or about what Christ has done for us. Rather, in real time we enter into the *presence* of the risen and ascended Christ. This means that we are not merely encountering our Bibles or the church or whatever means by which Christ might be present to us. We meet Christ. It is, to use technical language, an unmediated encounter.

In the Old Testament, we think of Moses' encounter with the burning bush (Ex 3) or Isaiah's encounter with the glory of God (Is 6). In the New Testament, we of course are deeply taken with the wide range of encounters with Christ described in the Gospels. What makes those accounts so significant to us is not merely that they are fascinating Bible stories. Rather, through the grace of the Spirit this Christ revealed in the Gospels is now the very Christ who we meet, most notably in our prayers and in worship. It is the very same Christ Jesus. Just as he was present to the disciples, to Martha and Mary, and to Nicodemus, he is now present to each one of us. Spiritual direction is about making sense of this encounter with the risen Christ—recognizing the presence of Christ and attending to the grace of Christ in our lives.

Because the Spirit was poured out at Pentecost, this grace—the encounter with Christ, in real time—is available to every Christian. This capacity is exquisitely profiled in the words of 2 Corinthians 3:18, where the apostle writes, "And we all, with unveiled face, beholding the glory of the Lord, are being transformed into the same image from one degree of glory to another. For this comes from the Lord who is the Spirit" (ESV).

Furthermore, as Paul observes in 2 Corinthians, this is a *transforming* encounter. Through the grace of the Spirit, we meet Christ and are transformed into the image of Christ. The theological principle is so very crucial here. Our transformation comes not by the strength of our resolve or by the diligence of our spiritual discipline or by the quality of our religious practices; rather it is the gracious work of Christ, who by his Spirit is drawing us to himself and transforming us into his image. Neither is our transformation merely the outworking of our understanding certain biblical principles and applying them diligently to our lives. We certainly do need resolve and spiritual discipline. And we most assuredly should seek to know the wisdom of the Scriptures and then live in the light of what we have learned. But the heart of the matter is a personal, real-time encounter with Christ Jesus. It is the experience of Christ that transforms.

In other words, just as the people described in the Gospels had the opportunity to meet Christ and know him, personally and intimately, this same grace and opportunity is, through the gift of the Spirit, available to each Christian. Even more, we enter into this encounter longing to be more and more *like* Christ, even as we are drawn into a deeper union *with* Christ.

The essence of spiritual direction is to foster this capacity for transformation. Directees enter into this ministry as those who seek to grow in faith, hope and love. And yet the sequence is important: spiritual growth is the fruit of an encounter with Christ. And, typically, it is an encounter through prayer— which is why later in this book I will stress that spiritual direction is very much about fostering the capacity for prayer or, better put, for knowing and meeting Christ in prayer. Transformation itself, then, is the byproduct of knowing Christ, of being drawn into the presence of Christ.

But then, in all of this affirmation of immediacy, we need to ask: where is religious experience *located*? The Old Testament Psalms suggest that religious experience is located in the heart. For example, we read:

Take delight in the LORD,
> and he will give you the desires of your heart. (Ps 37:4)

Create in me a clean heart, O God,
> and put a new and right spirit within me. (Ps 51:10)

Search me, O God, and know my heart;
> test me and know my thoughts. (Ps 139:23)

Clearly the language of the heart attests to the interior life, including but not limited to one's innermost thoughts. The church throughout her history has also recognized the significance of the "affections"—which speaks as much as anything to what is happening us to emotionally.

This way of thinking about the life of faith as centered in the heart was evident not only to the sixteenth-century "southern" Reformers, including Ignatius Loyola, but also to the great revival preachers of the eighteenth century, including John Wesley and Jonathan Edwards. Religion was for them a matter of the heart: the ordering of desire, the cultivation of emotional resilience and the fostering of joy.

All of this presumes that what is happening to us emotionally is not secondary to our spiritual experience, but may actually be—pun intended—the heart of the matter. Spiritual directors recognize that joy and sorrow, desolation and consolation, are critical indicators of the presence and work of the Spirit in our lives. And they recognize that few things are so crucial to our growth in faith, hope and love as our capacity to be alert to the emotional contours of our lives.

It is not that good doctrine does not matter, and we are not for a moment pitting heart and head against one another. Neither are we suggesting that clear and sound judgments—compelling logic and careful reasoning—are not important. Of course they are. But when we ask about the movement of the Spirit in our lives, the data to which we attend is the movement of the heart. We ask the questions, What is happening to us emotionally? Where is there sorrow or joy? What does this mean and what does it suggest to us about the work of the Spirit in our lives?

In other words, we do not buy into the more modern notion that emotion speaks of superficiality, and that the most rational people are the deepest people. Rather, the depth of our hearts reflects the depth of our emotional lives; nothing so captures the inner recesses of our beings as what is happening to us emotionally. Yes, there are superficial and passing feelings. But the genius of good direction is that we probe together, director and directee, and attend to the emotional wake that is left by the myriad of experiences we have had or are having. Here we find the data, the testimony, to the witness of the Spirit in our hearts and in our lives.

Now, as part of a fundamental theological perspective we must stress two things here—two things that are indispensable to our understanding of religious experience. First, we must speak of the religious and spiritual dimension of all aspects of life. While we certainly have explicitly and specifically religious or spiritual experiences, what we urgently need to see and feel is the presence of God in the whole of our lives and experiences—in each relationship, in each task we engage, in our leisure and in our play, in our sleep and in our waking. And second, this point also reminds us that we need to foster an appreciation of the power and significance of the ordinary and the mundane, and the presence of God in seasons of quiet and stillness. We learn to recognize the value of weeding gardens, and washing dishes, and running errands, and waiting to go through security as we board a flight. We come to see that the presence of God in our lives may not be found solely in a mountaintop experience, but also in the extended train trip, or a season of waiting for the restoration of health—a time when we simply wait and learn to be still.

THE PARTICULARITY OF EACH PERSON

When we speak of a theology of spiritual direction, it is also important to stress that each person is unique. Effective spiritual direction recognizes the particularity of a person's life and journey. A director does not impose his or her agenda, or experience, on the directee. The agenda and timing for the transforming work of God in this life, in this person, is set by Christ himself. And so we are attentive to the Spirit of Christ, and to the ways in which the Spirit is calling for repentance and learning and growth and maturity in this person at this time. We do not impose an agenda on the Spirit but attend to how the Spirit is calling—not in a general or generic way, but particularly. We certainly are governed in our thinking and pastoral care by biblical principles, but with the Scriptures as an essential context and backdrop, we listen to how the Spirit is calling this person, at this time, to respond to the wisdom of Christ.

For John of the Cross, in *Living Flame of Love*, this is *the* great danger in spiritual direction: that a director might presume, on the basis of his or her experience or from convictions gained through the reading of Scripture, to know God's call or intent in the directee's life, work and relationships.[1]

We cannot presume to know, and in the end we cannot know—for the witness of the Spirit is to the heart of the directee alone. Some insist that one can receive a word—perhaps a "prophetic" word—for the other. And yet, while we might certainly have a clear sense that there is something we need to offer another person, we must tread carefully and bring our observations tentatively, knowing that in the end the significance of what we are offering can only be known and appreciated by the other to whom we speak. It is not for us to judge. In the end, only the directee is able to discern and recognize the call of God for his or her life. As directors, we listen and consider with the directee, How is God present to you at this time? Many come for direction eager to have the director tell them what to do. They want guidance; perhaps they even want someone else, who they see as older and wiser, to hear God for them. But the wisdom of spiritual direction is precisely that we refuse to stand between God and the person who so needs to hear God for himself, for herself.

So I must make this so very vital point: spiritual direction is a ministry that fosters and encourages personal responsibility. We foster not dependence, but a growing maturity in Christ—the capacity of the directee to respond to Christ not through another, but on their own terms as they grow into and within an adult faith in Christ.

As the directee, *you* need to discern and recognize what God is saying to you, at this time, in this place, at this point in *your* life. Others, including a spiritual director, hopefully might provide some assistance in this essential discernment process. But in the end, we each take personal responsibility for what we sense God is saying to us. And it is my impression that the Spirit is typically calling us to grow in one area of our lives at a time. I remember when Father Tom Green mentioned this to me when he was serving as my director. I assured him that while that principle was perhaps acceptable for some, God would likely need to multitask in my situation, since there were so many areas of needed growth in my life! His gracious response was so simple and wise: "Gordon, God has all of eternity to transform you into the image of his Son; the question is, where is God at work and what is the priority of the Spirit in your life right now?"

We all long for transformation and growth, and this requires that we learn to trust the Spirit and be attentive to the Spirit's agenda and timing. Spiritual direction is a ministry of co-discernment: helping us recognize the immediate agenda of the Spirit. And it is the immediate agenda of the Spirit in this one life. We come to the ministry of direction making no assumptions about the priority of our experience, and we are very careful not to assume that we have "seen this one before." This is precisely why spiritual direction is typically a personal and individual experience. Every single person is on an individual journey.

God is at work, personally and individually, in the life of each one of us. We each need to make sense for ourselves of the way in which God is present—calling, encouraging and fostering greater growth in faith, hope and love. In direction, we let God be God—both with respect to God's agenda and to the timing of that agenda. What is the intent of God for this person at this time?

THE CHURCH: THE PEOPLE OF GOD

Our lives are organically a part of the people of God, the body of Christ. Another vital theological principle is that a spiritual director comes to this ministry as a representative of the church, in the name of Christ but also as a brother or sister, as a fellow pilgrim on the road, as one with us in the community of faith.

In the Christian life we each are in immediate communion with Christ, personally and individually. Further, we each must take responsibility for our encounter with Christ and our growth in faith. And yet while these two affirmations are true, we must also quickly add that we are not alone. We have companions on the road, others who accompany us and are to us a means of Christ's grace in our lives. We are part of a faith community. And a spiritual director comes into an individual's life circumstances as a representative of that community.

Christ gives us multiple gifts along the way. Particularly, Paul speaks of "gifts" such as apostles, prophets, evangelists and pastor-teachers who equip us and foster within us the capacity to grow up in Christ (Eph 4:11). The spiritual director is such a gift—while not, as indicated earlier, an indispensable gift, for many it is an *invaluable* gift from Christ to have a companion in the journey by means of this ministry.

Whether we have an actual spiritual director or not, we need others as a check and balance in our spiritual journey. This is so for a number of reasons. We each have a significant capacity for self-deception, for rationalizing our behavior, even for self-destructive behavior. We need others who love and accept us but who are able to speak graciously and without flattery regarding the specifics of our lives.

We are so easily crushed by criticism, and we are so inclined to have inflated heads when we receive some measure of praise. The friend, or spiritual director, comes alongside to help us moderate what is happening to us emotionally, precisely so that we take criticism for what it is—a potential for growth and learning—and take affirmation for no more than it is—a helpful marker along the way. We don't let either go to our head. Few things are so insidious to the spiritual life as pride. It is very nearly impossible to navigate the rough and tumble of the spiritual life without another, who comes alongside, to keep us humble. And one sign of this humility is that we are not crushed by criticism or flattered by praise. It is very nearly impossible, if not actually impossible, to get a good read on ourselves—to take a sober look at ourselves (see Rom 12:3)—without an external guide, be that a good friend or a spiritual director, who will keep us from overstating our weaknesses or being overly self-impressed with our capacities. The other helps us actually see our weaknesses and potential vulnerabilities that could come to haunt us in a time of stress or difficulty. Also, when we are trying to make sense of a significant experience, particularly one that leaves an emotional wake—whether it be a difficult experience that leaves us in anger or discouragement, or a more positive one where something went very well and we received affirmation and praise—we need another to help us make sense of what is happening to us. This can certainly come through good friends. But the ministry of spiritual direction formalizes this input and assures us that it will happen. Indeed, I would in the end suggest we need both—both the very best of friendship and wise, informed spiritual direction.

We are deeply emotional creatures—all of us. And emotions are powerful forces, for good and ill. Deep sorrow, while surely appropriate in response to loss, can so easily discombobulate us. Anger, in the face of a grave wrong, so easily leads to bitterness. Discouragement and disappointment, left unchecked, can so easily result in cynicism. And fear, so easily rationalized as a "concern" for another, can overcome our capacity to think and respond courageously to a challenge we are facing. The huge gift of the other who walks alongside us in our faith journey, is that of responding graciously to our circumstances with apt words and, as needed, gentle correction. Effective spiritual direction fosters emotional self-awareness, including the freedom to acknowledge and name our anger, our fear and our discouragement. But then also, an effective director does not allow us to stay there, mired in our anger and sorrow. We can so easily feel overcome by guilt, fear, sorrow and darkness; we need the other to point out the light and signs of God's goodness and presence in the midst of this darkness when we are so easily blinded by our own emotions.

In addition, we all need encouragement. In our lives and work and relationships we are so easily discouraged and disheartened. A wise spiritual director is able to see the subtle ways in which we need to be encouraged and renewed in hope. And their insight is to speak an apt word—not so much "let me encourage you," but the appropriate word for this person at this time in the face of this disheartening situation.

The "other" in our life is essential to our capacity to know Christ and respond to Christ with patience and courage. Part of the great genius of the Christian understanding of religious experience is found in this remarkable counterpoint: we are individuals before God, but we are not alone in this encounter with God. We need one another to live with vitality and strength and hope. The Christian life is not self-sustainable.

I think, for example, of the eager and open Ethiopian who headed south, trying to make sense of the words of the prophet Isaiah. God, through the Spirit, sent him Philip to interpret the text for him but then also to help him process the appropriate response to what he was seeing in that text—the Messiah of Israel, the Lord Jesus Christ, into whom, through Philip, the Ethiopian would be baptized (Acts 8:26-39).

I also think of those who preside over and lead our worship—the calling of the liturgist. Here too we have a role or ministry of one who is not the goal or object of our worship—that object is Christ and Christ alone, and we are drawn into worship by the Spirit and through Christ we bring glory and honor and praise to the Father. But though the focus and sustaining energy of worship is God and God alone, this does not make liturgical leadership dispensable. As we each come to worship, together with the people of God, we need those who are called to preside and lead and prompt us in our worship to "direct" our minds and hearts to Christ in response to the prompting of the Spirit. We need those who can bring the wisdom of the church's history of worship to bear on this time of worship.

In like manner a spiritual director comes into our circumstances in the name of Christ, not as Christ per se, but very much as the gift of Christ to us and thus as Christ for us, as one from within the faith community, the church, who comes alongside to gently correct, encourage and guide. We need another to bring a word of discernment, another who will draw on the ancient biblical and historical wisdom of the church in a way that is apt and appropriate and timely.

The stress on the ministry of the other—the director—as one who comes into our lives as part of the ministry of the church to the individual Christian is also a reminder that spiritual direction presupposes a life in Christian community. The strength and value of spiritual direction is precisely as a ministry that complements the full-orbed life and ministry of the church. As a general rule, we can assume that those who receive direction are also participating in the ministry of the Word—the teaching and preaching of the Scriptures, most notably within the context of Christian worship. Further, as a director I assume that the one receiving direction is either moving toward baptism or, in direction, seeking to live out their full baptismal identity. Baptism is a crucial benchmark in the spiritual life.

This finds expression as well in one's full participation in the regular celebration of the Lord's Supper. This might surprise some, particularly those whose worship includes only occasional celebrations of the Lord's Supper. But no doubt many recognize that a full appreciation of the sacramental life of the church includes a recognition of the vital place of the Lord's Supper—Holy Communion, the Eucharist—in the life of the church and in the life of the individual Christian. And I would concur: the bread and cup are an indispensable means of grace, an essential counterpart to the interiority that is fostered through spiritual direction.

Then also, spiritual direction assumes that one is finding ways and means for fruitful service, both within Christian community and as one who with others is in service, in mission, within one's local community but also with an attentiveness to the work of God around the world. Spiritual direction is, without apology, a ministry that is focused on one person. For the directee, this is a time to ask about one's own journey of faith, giving attention to the state of one's own soul. There is an inward focus; the director helps us make sense of our own selves and our own experience of God's grace, including our own emotional ups and downs. We are, for the moment at least, self-focused. And yet the agenda is not one that fosters self-centeredness. To the contrary, our reflection on ourselves is but a means to foster our capacity for full engagement in the purposes of God—the mission of God—in the world. We foster self-focus so that we can grow in our capacity to live not self-centered lives, but other-centered lives. And thus participation in the life and ministry of the church—through generous service—is an essential counterpoint to the ministry of spiritual direction.

There is no doubt that many who come for spiritual direction will speak of frustration and even disillusionment with the church. And they may feel rather marginal to the church and actually view direction as a kind of substitute for being part of a congregation of Christian believers. While there may be times when some distance from the formal life of the church might be appropriate, it can only be—at most—for a season, and ideally for a brief season. Spiritual direction is a ministry that arises out of the life of the church and that, in turn, fosters our capacity to live in mutual dependence within Christian community. It is a ministry of the church, and it is a ministry that assumes our full participation in the life of the church, for it is a ministry that complements the other dimensions of congregational life.

Bringing together these theological perspectives, William A. Barry has a superb reflection on the place of spiritual direction. He writes:

> Reflection on our experience reveals the mysterious presence of God who is always acting to draw us into community with the Trinity and with one another; this community is the Kingdom of God and its bond is the

Holy Spirit poured out into our hearts. Fear and egocentrism lead us to resist God's action, and spiritual direction is a singularly appropriate ministry to help us overcome our fears.[2]

That captures it wonderfully. Spiritual direction is a ministry that engages our deepest selves—notably at the point of our fears—and equips us to respond to the work of the Spirit through whom we are being drawn into the life of the triune God and into the life of the community of faith, the church. This wonderful presence of God in our lives and in the world is truly a benevolent presence; recognizing and, indeed, feeling the force of this love is crucial to our response. Thus, as often as not, a spiritual director will seek to draw out our awareness of the goodness of God, the God who is worthy of our unbounded praise and thanksgiving. We learn to respond to God who is indeed present to each aspect and dimension of our lives; we find God in our prayers and worship, of course, but what emerges is that we learn to see God in all things.

3

Focused Conversation

Spiritual direction can certainly be offered informally—in conversation along the way, with colleagues and friends, a pastor with a parishioner, or a teacher with a student—as we offer a listening ear and make observations and suggestions in response to what we have heard. I will speak to these other settings later. But as I am speaking of direction in this chapter, I am picturing a *formal* relationship specifically for the purpose of a *focused* conversation.

It is my experience, and that of many others, that this might typically be for an hour and, perhaps quite intentionally, no more than an hour. By choosing to meet for an hour, we keep the time focused. Further, the meeting is regular: perhaps director and directee meet every three or four weeks, or perhaps even less frequently, but it is a regular meeting so that much of the value or fruit of the spiritual conversation comes as the two have opportunity to journey together over a longer stretch of time.

It is a focused, regular, intentional conversation.

But now to address the *content* of this conversation: What do we attend to? What do we talk about? In spiritual direction, there is a double listening. We attend to what is presented, the specific themes or matters for reflection and sharing. And then, in and through what is on the table, we attend to what Christ is communicating to us by the Spirit. But still, there is conversation; and to make our attentiveness to the Spirit most fruitful, we need to foster the kind or character of conversation that will facilitate our objective in direction: to know the inner witness of the Spirit.

As we come together to this awareness, it is most fruitful if the directee can speak about some very specific dimensions of his or her life. It is not necessary to go into great detail, though in some circumstances it might be necessary to provide significant background information for an issue at hand. But as a rule, this is what I seek from my directees: in each case, attending in particular to their joys and sorrows as the primary data by which we are alert to the presence of the Spirit.

RELATIONSHIPS AND WORK

A director typically suggests, "Tell me about your key relationships—and where in these relationships there is joy and, of course, where there is sorrow, stress, disappointment and perhaps disillusionment." And, "Tell me about your work—not just paid, salaried work, but the work to which you are called, your responsibilities and duties, whether at home or in the marketplace, whether in salaried work or in the raising of children, and where in your work you are experiencing joy or sorrow, stress or frustration, setback or the opening up of new possibilities and challenges."

Along the way, a director asks further about the joys and sorrows that inevitably arise from our relationships and our work. And we consider, What does this joy or this sorrow mean? What might God be saying through this particular point of sorrow or stress or joy? We look at our key relationships and work, affiliations and associations on the one hand, and our responsibilities and duties on the other. And we pay attention. It is this very paying attention that allows us to grow in wisdom. We mature in wisdom not merely by reading the Bible and engaging ancient truth. We also grow in wisdom as we see and know ourselves and recognize the particularity of God's work in our lives. We know our own story and thus we know ourselves as we see ourselves through the lens of God's presence and work in us.

The great gift of a spiritual director is to help us pay attention and interpret, as best as we can, the significance—for our growth in faith, hope and love—of points of joy and sorrow as they intersect our lives. A spiritual director helps us to see these as having meaning, and in the process to consider where the Spirit is leaving a trace of God's presence in our lives. As noted, the trace of God's presence in our lives is found in that emotional wake—the joys and sorrows we have experienced along the way.

In spiritual direction, a director helps the other make sense of their religious experience. By *religious* we mean not religious activities per se, but rather that we are attentive to the ways in which the whole of our lives are infused, potentially, with the presence of God. Thus in all aspects and dimensions of our lives, we need to be attentive to the presence of God, the grace of God and the call of God.

A KEY DECISION IN A TIME OF CHOICE

A spiritual director is also an invaluable resource when we are facing a significant decision or choice. A director is typically most able to serve us if the relationship has some history, where the director comes to know us quite well since the journey together has gone on for a number of years. Whether it is in respect to our relationships or our work, we often face choices — perhaps a decision of whether we will marry this person, or whether we will accept the offer of a job. Our lives are filled with so many choices and decisions and it is invaluable to be able to invite a spiritual director to listen in as we make sense of decisions that shape the contours of our lives, that set the direction for the upcoming chapters of our lives.

Here is where it is imperative that the spiritual director is someone who does not have a vested interest in the outcome of the decision that we are facing: the director needs to be able to listen and consider and, hopefully, confirm that indeed we are choosing well. Or, if there are significant factors that are not being considered, the director must be able to graciously ask probing questions and raise a perspective that might add light to the decision-making process.

It is so very important to stress that the spiritual director does not make a decision for us and might not even counsel us one way or the other. A true spiritual director will resist any inclination to tell us what they think might be best for us, one way or the other. Their passion and longing is for us to know, from Christ himself, the call of God in our lives. And they will not interfere with this vital and life-giving word from the Lord! They will not risk that years later we might say: my director told me to marry John, or to quit my job. No chance of this. A spiritual director, however much they may have a good read on our situation, knows that the power of call and effective decision making resides precisely in the wonder that we hear the voice of Jesus ourselves.

Sometimes, also, a spiritual director might suggest an alternate implication to something we are facing. Recently I met with someone who was discerning whether he and his wife were to leave their church because of their intense longing to be part of a more liturgical and historical church tradition. As I listened to them, I acknowledged that indeed, perhaps God was leading them to move down the so-called Canterbury trail. But then I wondered with them if another possibility was that God would actually want them to stay with their current fellowship, and perhaps on regular occasions drop in for worship in an Anglican church so that that side of their heart longing and formation is nurtured. But I only offered the suggestion, the possibility. I will listen in on the decision-making process, but only so that I can foster their capacity to hear, from the Lord himself, how God would have them act, with grace and courage.

As a rule, the observations and suggestions of a spiritual director are offered tentatively and with qualification; they do not presume to speak for God or presume that their words are precisely what God is saying to this person at this time. What directors long for in directees that is that we would hear God for ourselves, and not need to depend on another to hear God's word for us. A director comes alongside, to listen and perhaps to help us interpret and make sense of the issues at hand and particularly the joys or sorrows that might accompany this decision-making process.

When in anger we are tempted to quit a job, a director will urge us to choose in peace and not in desolation—essentially moderating our response to what is perhaps a difficult situation. When we are being drawn into a situation or an opportunity, the director can provide us with another set of eyes and ears, another perspective on what lies before us. They can ask, "So what is it that draws you to this person (perhaps in a marriage opportunity), or to this job offer?" And they can help us test and confirm that our intentions and desires are rooted in the good and the noble and the excellent (see Phil 4:8).

It is also important to stress that good directors are not necessarily impressed with grand schemes or dramatic "Damascus road" experiences of call. They will encourage us to move slowly and test and confirm that the movement of our hearts is truly from God. You may feel a deep and powerful call to be a missionary to the farthest reaches of the world. Fine! But your director will foster your capacity to test this call, to see that it is indeed arising from God and from the purposes of God for your life. Directors will not assume that a more "religious" call is necessarily superior or more likely to come from God than a call to the ordinary and the simple. They will not assume that a call to a distant land is to take priority over a call to the local and what is immediately at hand.

But in all of this, the important thing to stress is that a director will help us discern well. A director will not discern the call and purposes of God for us, but will help us discern for ourselves.

And yet, there may be a crisis situation; someone may be about to move into a marriage relationship that is clearly going to be abusive and in which they have clearly not discerned well. Or perhaps someone is about to make a decision that anyone looking in would recognize is not only unsuitable but will lead to much suffering and disappointment.

At times like this it is imperative that the spiritual director speak openly, frankly and, we trust, appropriately. A director owes it to the other to speak as directly as possible and to indicate that as we are contemplating the possibility of a life-shaping choice, it all seems very suspect or not adequately prayed through or thought through. We are entering into a decision or a relationship for all the wrong reasons. And so the director must speak. Yet this is not the ideal or the norm; very rarely does a director choose to speak for God—rarely, and I am suggesting, only in crisis situations. And they recognize that each time they make such an intervention it is actually a step back. Directors intervene and in the process actually undercut our capacity to listen to God for ourselves. This must be the long-term goal—that directees grow in the capacity to hear God themselves. Intervention may be offered, but rarely and only to avert a crisis.

SUFFERING AND PAIN

For many, the journey of faith is marked by suffering, setback and disappointment. This will also, of course, be a topic for reflection. I say "for many," but the book of Hebrews in the New Testament suggests that difficulty, indeed suffering, will be the mark of all true followers of Christ. Jesus himself was perfected by suffering (Heb 2:10); and the clear indication of the book of Hebrews is that pain, suffering and difficulty will intersect the life of each sincere seeker after God.

A spiritual director will naturally want to offer comfort, compassion and sympathy. And yet the most crucial offering, if this comfort and compassion can be found elsewhere, is for the director to still be a co-discerner—not so much caught up in the pain and disappointment as with compassion, certainly, but most of all with quietness of heart and equanimity of spirit to help the directee respond to the question: "So, in this difficulty and darkness when God seems so absent, can we begin to consider what God is trying to say and offer to you through this?"

The spiritual director helps us interpret our experience by offering an alternative perspective or read of our situation and circumstance. I remember vividly while in a direction conversation expressing frustration with some colleagues—looking, I admit, for some sympathy! But my director's response was so simple and clear: "Well, Gordon, it is sometimes helpful to remember that 'difficult people are the faculty of the soul,' and perhaps they are, in a way, a gift to you to help you grow in patience." I wanted sympathy, and I thought I could use an empathetic ear. But my need was to see the situation differently. And the role of the director was simply to see how God might be actually present to my situation.

It is so important that the spiritual director offer words of encouragement and renewed hope. We are easily discouraged in our relationships and our work. Part of listening is that we are attentive to the points of hope and grace in the midst of the darkness.

When there is joy in our life and work, the spiritual director is present to speak words that remind us of the need for thanksgiving—lest any feeling of entitlement or self-satisfaction arise in our hearts. In times of sorrow and discouragement, we need words of hope—lest our anger become bitterness, lest our discouragement become cynicism. We need another to speak the words that check any propensity we might have to be overcome by our sorrows, any propensity they might have to take root within us.

Sometimes a spiritual director may help us see that the way before us is closed—that we need to accept this reality. As I sometimes jokingly suggest, when a directee is seeking to discern whether to marry John or not, the director's wisdom at that moment might be nothing more profound than the obvious: Well, John married Mary last week, so perhaps we need to take another tack in our discernment process! We need to see and name our reality—our circumstances and situations as they actually are, not as we wish they were. But just as often, a spiritual director can help us be sure that we have not overstated the meaning of setback or failure, but can rather come out of this setback with renewed vision and hope.

And when we are discouraged, we do not need platitudes and banalities. Spiritual directors of course affirm that God is good and God's mercies endure. But do so with particular reference to the directee's circumstances and to the particular ways in which God is demonstrating his goodness and faithfulness for this person at this time in life. We do not need generalities; we need specifics. This is part of why spiritual direction is so formative: the director brings words of insight and hope into the particularities of *this* person's life, at this time, in this season, in the face of this particular set of disappointments and challenges.

Now, of course, the directee may not accept these words of encouragement and hope; we may be so overcome by discouragement that we cannot let go of despair. In those times, directors offer what they sense God is calling them to offer; they say what they think God would have them say. But in the end, they accept that each one needs to take adult responsibility for our own life. Each needs to attend to their own response to the circumstances of life. This is a reminder that in spiritual direction, directors let go of the need for immediate results—or the gratification of feeling that they have made an immediate and substantive difference in the life of another.

Directors plant seeds. They water seeds. But the Spirit gives the growth. They trust God to do God's work in God's time, and accept the limits of what they can offer in this conversation at this time and at this place. A spiritual director is not a hero or a miracle worker, but merely one who listens and, as appropriate, speaks what will be an apt word in season. They leave the fruit of their work to the hands of God. And to the timing of God.

In chapter one I stressed that we must distinguish between teaching and spiritual direction. Teaching may address the universals of our faith, and direction, as the complement to teaching, considers the specific application in one person's life—in the relationships and work of the directee. And yet, there are times for directors when a teaching moment might be appropriate—for example, clarifying a passage of Scripture that has been misread, where a more accurate reading might give clarity and new and appropriate direction. I think, perhaps, of someone who discounts work in the kitchen from a reading of the Martha and Mary story, where a more helpful reading could clarify what it is that Jesus is really saying to Martha. The essential meaning of this text is not that prayer is superior to the active life, but rather that Martha was consumed with worry—note the central focus of Jesus' comments to her: "Martha, Martha, you are worried and distracted by many things" (Lk 10:41).

At other times, the spiritual director needs to gently challenge a false understanding of God. Most frequently in this regard, I find that I need to remind directees that God is benevolent and full of mercy, kind and generous, for them and not against them. And yet, while this is a kind of teaching, it is teaching that comes in the form of a reminder, a gentle corrective, that arises in direct response to the circumstances of the directee's life—and it is offered more by way of drawing on ancient wisdom for the occasion, rather than a brief lecture offered as part of a lesson plan.

One might say that through spiritual direction we foster a capacity for what students of human thinking call meta-cognition. Spiritual direction fosters the capacity not just for thinking—cognition—but also to step back and see oneself from the outside: to think about thinking, specifically one's own intellectual and emotional processes. Metacognition is to become self-aware and to be able to ask, What's happening here, in my own heart and mind? What am I feeling? What does it mean? What am I learning? And, most of all, where is God in all of this?

4

Attending to What Is Happening in Our Prayers

Nothing is more fundamental to the spiritual life than the capacity to pray, and nothing is more central to spiritual direction than attending to what is happening in our prayers.

This does not mean that the focus of conversation in spiritual direction is our prayers. It might be, but that is not necessarily the case. Typically, as already discussed, the focus of our conversation will be our relationships and work, with particular reference to suffering and difficulty—the stress points of our lives—and with reference to times of choice. Yet prayer is nevertheless a primary reference point, even if unstated. I am not including prayer as necessarily one of the topics for conversation in spiritual direction. It might be, of course, and it will be if the spiritual director has particular concerns about the quality of the directee's prayers. But it will not necessarily be something to which we give special attention.

And yet it is crucial to understand that one comes to a spiritual director as a pray-er. In many respects, spiritual direction is the ministry that assists us to make sense of what is happening in our prayers.

While the whole of life matters—our work, relationships, everything—what gives the whole of life meaning is that we see and enter into each dimension of our lives as those—to use a phrase that Paul uses repeatedly in Ephesians 1—who are "in Christ." Just as the church is first and foremost a liturgical community and engaged in the world as those who are first and foremost a community of worshipers, while prayer is not the whole of our lives, it is indispensable to our capacity to truly be who we are called to be in the world. When we neglect our prayers, we in effect secularize our lives. As pray-ers, we have the potential, at least, to see our entire lives in terms of the purposes, calling and presence of God in our world and in our lives.

Jesus' life and ministry only makes sense when we appreciate that he was a pray-er (see Mk 1:35-42). So it is no surprise that his disciples turned to him and asked him to teach them how to pray. Why does this matter? Because the genius of spiritual direction, the heart of the matter, is fostering the capacity of this person to be in Christ, in union with Christ. This implies that spiritual direction is about fostering the capacity of this person to pray.

ELEMENTS OF GROWTH IN PRAYER

Spiritual direction is often provided in the context of prayer or prayer retreats. With those I direct, I have found it fruitful to meet in connection with a day of prayer or following a retreat, to listen in as they reflect on the experience of God in their prayers.

This means, of course, that through the ministry of spiritual direction we are fostering the capacity to pray well—to mature in our prayers and in our inclination to pray. For the beginner in the spiritual life, spiritual direction needs to include either an intentional orientation to prayer or, at the very least, assurance that the directee is receiving appropriate instruction in the practice of prayer. What a gift it was to me in my young adult years to have the opportunity to meet with my pastor, Alex Aronis, an hour a week over ten weeks to introduce me to the approach to prayer found in the *Spiritual Exercises* of Ignatius Loyola. I think back with deep gratitude that this was a pastor with a vision to teach parishioners how to pray, and he was prepared to teach them one on one, one by one. He was never so busy or preoccupied with church management that he did not have time for this very basic dimension of pastoral ministry. Yes, it takes time, but it may be one of the most powerful gifts we can give another—teaching them how to pray.

For beginners, elemental instruction may well be necessary. For more mature Christians, our prayers, while not taken for granted in direction, serve as the backdrop by which we make sense of what is happening to us in our relationships, in our work, through the joys and sorrows and stresses of life. A good director will be attentive to what is happening in the prayers of the directee through how the directee is speaking about the various dimensions of life and work and relationships.

We need to stress that in speaking about prayer in this particular context, I mean not intercessory prayer per se—prayer as the longings and heartfelt expressions of God's people for the mercy and intervention of God in our lives and in our world. Rather, I am speaking of prayer here as first of all communion with Christ, in real time, and second as the capacity to listen and be attentive to the presence of God in our lives and, specifically, in our prayers. In our prayers we certainly do speak to God, but we listen more than we speak, and we learn to be present to Christ and to find our deep joy in this presence.

Yet this does not suggest there is no order. Even in our personal, intimate and private prayers, there is often a liturgy, an order, with the classic elements of prayer that we recognize in the Old Testament Psalms, the prayers of Jesus and the spiritual heritage of the Christian church. As spiritual directors, we need to have some assurance that the directee is a pray-er. As we help others make sense of their lives, we are attentive to what is happening in their prayers. Typically we would want some assurance or evidence of several factors—and if these are not present, then the work of direction would properly seek to encourage these elements: (1) that in prayer, the directee is growing in gratitude—the capacity for thanksgiving, for attending to the multiple ways in which God is demonstrating his love and goodness to them; (2) that in prayer, the directee has the capacity for confession and repentance, for turning from sin and embracing the righteous call of God on their life.

On this second point, though, an important caveat. Many of us come from religious subcultures that are, for lack of a better word, guilt ridden. And it is easy to come to a spiritual director so very conscious of all ways in which we have fallen short. We feel badly that we have not been all that we should be, and in meeting with the director, we can easily list off these various *perceived* sins, failures and shortcomings.

One of the gifts of spiritual direction is to help us sift through all of this guilt and foster our capacity to discern a key question: While we are certainly not all that we are ultimately called to be, specifically where is God calling us to turn now, at this point in our lives? This leads us to think not so much of sins that need to be confessed, but rather points of growth and development, learning and formation, to which we are being called. Sin is no doubt a factor in our lives, and confession is most appropriate in the context of the ministry of spiritual direction. It is a false comfort when the spiritual director does not recognize with us the depth of our need to turn from sin to spiritual health. Ignoring sin in spiritual direction is as absurd as a medical doctor ignoring the presence of sickness. Yes, there is sin and failure in our lives, certainly, but since God has all of eternity to transform us into the image of his Son, we are freed to ask the pivotal question in direction: Now, at this time and juncture in my life and work, where is God calling me to grow in grace, turn from sickness and sin, and mature in faith, hope and love?

Then the director also needs the assurance (3) that in prayer, the Scriptures are playing a dynamic role in the renewing of the directee's mind, the shaping of conscience and the formation of a Christian imagination. Here too, the director needs some assurance that we know how to read the Bible, or, better put, that we know how to listen to God through the witness of the Scriptures. Again, a director may not be the one who teaches us how to read the Scriptures, but the director can only effectively co-discern with us if the Scriptures are an integral dimension of our lives and specifically of our prayers.

Finally, (4) that the directors will be attentive to whether directees have the capacity to discern how God is providing guidance and direction. This means that in the conversation the director is able to ask: So, in the midst of this challenge or situation or difficulty or opportunity, what do you sense that Jesus is saying to you? And, while not always the case, as often as not this communication from Christ will come to us in our prayers.

While the focus of spiritual direction may not be our prayers, what is happening in our prayers is fundamental and is always the backdrop, the basic spiritual practice that allows us to see the whole of our lives in terms of the presence and grace of God.

WHEN PRAYER FEELS DRY

Before moving on, one more crucial point regarding prayer. As we mature in our prayers, we often feel disappointed or perplexed that our prayers have changed—particularly when we find that they do not seem as intense or emotionally satisfying as they once were. Perhaps we do not feel the deep comfort of Christ with the same kind of immediacy that we had when we were younger in the faith. Perhaps the Scriptures, while still very much the Word of God to us, do not jump out at us with the same power that we felt when we were first beginning in the Christian life. This could well be what spiritual writers like Teresa of Ávila speak of when she comments on the "dry well," or what John of the Cross calls the "dark night of the senses." These are powerful images that profile something that merits our attention: that as our prayers mature, they often if not always become less sensory. There is a quietness or a dryness that emerges. And often we are confused and wonder if something is wrong—if perhaps we have "lost our first love" and if we need to do something to "get the feeling back."

A wise director plays a critical role here, assuring us that this is the natural course of our prayers, the sign of God's gracious acceptance of growing maturity in prayer, where God no longer needs to pamper us or make us feel good. And in the end, this is not a loss; as both Teresa and John stress, our feelings can so easily get in the way of the deep work of God in our lives. The dryness in our prayers is not a sign of the absence of God but, perhaps, an indicator that God is actually very near at hand. In times like this a director needs merely to stress—to remind us—that we need to continue in our prayers and not dismiss them because they seem no longer fruitful. Then they remind us to test the quality of our prayers not by how we feel in prayer but by the fruit, the awareness of God's grace in our relationships and in our work.

When we are in the "dark night" in our prayers, we have two temptations. The first is to misread the situation and assume that something is wrong. The second is to run—to find some kind of emotional anesthetic, something to distract us from the deep work of God, whether it be television or anything that in effect renders our experience superficial. In both cases, a good spiritual director can bring our attention back to the necessary place of letting God do what only God can do when we learn to wait, even if it means learning to wait in the darkness.

Thus a spiritual director can play a key role in our lives and specifically in our growth in prayer. Without good direction, sincere people so easily assume that if God does not feel immediately present, that if they do not feel—and that is the operative word, *feel*—the immediate presence of God, then something must be wrong. And because they are sincere, they blame themselves. Since as a basic conviction of their lives they know that God is good and merciful, if they do not sense this immediate comfort from God it can only mean, they think, that they are not faithful enough in their lives and in their prayers.

A director will listen carefully at this point and, as I previously suggested, potentially play a critical role in responding to this dryness or darkness in our prayers. Perhaps, indeed, the problem is from our side: we have neglected our prayers, or the fundamental disciplines of the spiritual life. Perhaps, indeed, we have succumbed to pride and self-centeredness. Perhaps. And a director can gently call us back to an orientation of faith, hope and love and toward greater generosity in our disposition toward others and in our work. But as often as not, the genius of good direction at this point is the assurance that indeed God is present, but he is inviting us to live by faith and not by sight— calling us to be less dependent on the immediate sensory awareness of God's presence. The good director can assure us that all is well and that we can continue in our prayers and in the disciplines and service to which we are called, confident of God's love and providential care. A director can assure us that God's work continues in our lives, even if we do not feel this ministry of the Spirit quite like we did when we were beginners in the Christian life.

But the main point in all of this is that the essential backdrop to spiritual direction is the quality and character of our prayers. While not necessarily the focus of conversation, our prayers are vital to the spiritual life and to our capacity for spiritual growth. Further, the most fundamental relationship in our spiritual lives is not with the director but with God. The director can only have an effective ministry in our lives if in our prayers we are growing and maturing and learning and increasingly fostering our capacity to be attentive to Christ.

5

A Spiritual Direction Session

What is the nature of the actual session of formal spiritual direction? In chapter six I will highlight how spiritual direction can be integrated into other ministries, but here we will explore the hour where spiritual direction is the agenda at hand.

AN HOUR OF FOCUSED CONVERSATION

The reference to an hour is intentional and important. We recognize the sacredness of time and space as we step aside, from the demands of life and work, and from leisure and recreation, to consider how God is present to this person at this time.

While it is certainly possible to provide direction by telephone, this should ideally be the exception rather than the norm. As much as possible we meet in person, so that the whole of our communication—including the nonverbal—can be incorporated into our discernment.

In my experience, while a cup of coffee or tea at hand is certainly appropriate, it is best not to meet for direction over a meal or while on a walk. We might go for lunch together *after* our time of direction. And perhaps after lunch we might go for a walk together. But the time of direction requires a particular sensitivity, an alertness to the presence of the Spirit, such that we want a time and space with minimal distractions—no waiters interrupting our conversation, no cyclists scooting in front of us as we walk. Even if we are in a quiet park, walking itself can be an ever so slight distraction; there is something simple, elegant and powerful in sitting, with focused attention on this person at this time.

And it is a sacred hour. The cell phone and pager are turned off. Even the landline telephone is ignored, or ideally disconnected or put in mute mode. A do-not-disturb sign is placed on the door. Typically the most fruitful time in an hour of direction is in the second half of that hour, when we begin to distill from what has been said and offered what it is that we sense is of God. Nothing should disturb this process of attentiveness and discernment.

Perhaps we do not sit face to face across a table, but at an angle, as a way to sacramentally signal that while we are attentive to each other, there is Another to whom we both are giving ultimate attention. Some directors will light a candle—a simple but powerful sign, an ancient indicator in worship that now, in this time and in this place, Christ is with us.

How often do we meet? For the new Christian, who is just learning how to pray, it would not be inappropriate to meet every two or three weeks. For the mature Christian, it may well be that they only meet with a director three or four times a year. But either way, it is a consistent meeting and conversation where from one meeting to the next, we together grow—as directee and director—in our capacity to co-discern. There is no doubt that in my own experience, the most fruitful conversations with a spiritual director have come, as a rule, after we have met together over several years. Many times the most valuable insights come from a director who, after numerous meetings, over a period of time, is able to provide a comment with respect to a recurring theme that they identify as perhaps having significance in the directee's life.

THREE MOVEMENTS

When we meet for the hour of intentional, focused conversation, I find it helpful to think in terms of three phases or movements in this conversation.

First, the director listens as the one coming for direction speaks to the kinds of themes and issues that I mentioned earlier—the specific content and focus of our direction. This should be a concise account of the noteworthy markers in their life—typically what has brought joy or sorrow since the last meeting. I find it almost essential to ask that a person coming for direction take substantive time to prepare for our hour together, and to have in hand or even send me in advance a one-page outline with what they sense they are being asked to offer by way of observations about what is emerging for them in the faith journey.

The act of writing gives focus to our thoughts, helping us set aside the incidental—so that we are not distracted by what is not immediately pertinent. Writing helps give focus to those elements of our lives that most need to be highlighted in this conversation. To a directee, I offer the following: as you bring your reflections to your director, don't ramble aimlessly in your comments, but also be sure to provide enough nuance and texture to your observations that the director can get a feel for what is happening in your life. Avoid clichés and religious jargon, speak clearly and plainly. Avoid any pretense or any propensity to try to impress the spiritual director with the quality of your life and your piety! This is a safe space for honesty, frankness and humility. And don't feel any need to only speak about the dramatic and the emotionally charged; God's presence is often most evident in the ordinary and the mundane, the routine and the simple dimensions of our lives.

Second, the director responds—though perhaps allowing for a time of silence before speaking. Two or three minutes of silence are but another way of acknowledging, sacramentally, that we are in the presence of another. As directors, it is essential that we allow silence to be an aspect of our spiritual direction. Indeed, this should be stressed. We can alert the directee in advance that this will be part of our time together. After they have provided us with a reflection on their life situation and the matters that are coming to their attention, we tell them that a time of silence will follow. The director will not respond immediately, but in silence let what has been spoken sit and settle and be distilled in the presence of God. Silence is our friend, it is not an awkward moment in an otherwise engaging conversation. Indeed, silence should be viewed as an integral dimension of good conversation.

Then, out of a time of silence, the spiritual director responds. The response could be in two parts: first, perhaps, to ask some clarifying questions or enquire further into one part of the narrative that has just been offered. And second, having heard the directee's answers, to provide commentary and observations in Christ and as seems most appropriate to this person at this time. In my own experience as a directee I have often been impressed that my spiritual director did not feel the need to comment on everything I shared. I may have offered a narrative referring to four or five dimensions of my life that seemed to me significant. But typically the director would only comment on two or three and, indeed, sometimes on just one item that struck him as noteworthy.

And how might a spiritual director respond? What kinds of comments might be expected when one goes for direction? As noted in chapter two, directees seek a very particular grace: to respond well to the developments and circumstances of life—to respond with gratitude, with love and with a disposition of hope. All of this speaks of a response of faith, a deepening trust in the providential care of God and in God's guidance and direction in our lives.

Further, here or after additional response from the directee, the director may choose to offer suggestions for spiritual practice—to speak of the means of grace and the kinds of disciplines or practices or Scripture or spiritual readings that might be fruitful for the directee at this time. I have, for example, suggested the value of additional meditation on Scripture during Lent, or observed that perhaps the directee might find it fruitful to more frequently take part in the celebration of the Lord's Supper. When a person is feeling discouraged and crushed in the loss of employment or a crisis in their marriage, it is appropriate to urge that perhaps focused attention be given to immersion in the Scriptures or a more intentional approach to giving thanks in one's daily prayers.

In summary, first the directee speaks—taking twenty to thirty minutes, perhaps, to provide a focused reflection on the circumstances of their life (including the topics mentioned in chapter three). Second, the director responds, after a time of silence, taking ten to fifteen minutes to comment on what has been shared.

And finally, third, it is appropriate for a final and perhaps more brief exchange, where the directee provides comment and receives what has been offered by the director, perhaps clarifying and confirming that these words have been understood and accepted. After this response, the director may wish to comment further or simply leave it at that—as offered.

So we move through three phases during the hour of spiritual direction. Of course, it is eminently appropriate to take a few minutes either at the beginning or the end to offer a prayer—both a prayer of blessing by the director and a prayer of submission and faith by the directee.

In all of this it should be abundantly clear that good listening is the key to good direction. There is at work a grace of double listening. In spiritual direction, the director is attentive to what is offered in the narrative and account of the directee. As directors we pay attention; we have shut out the world, we have set aside our own cares and concerns, and we are present to this person—the directee—at this time. We listen, perhaps taking a note or two, but only to help us recall what is being offered—only to help us listen well.

But as the director listens, they are also attentive to the presence and work of the Spirit. We listen not in a way that second-guesses the directee, but rather in and through the words that are offered. A director is alert to how God is present and speaking. And this is why we are comfortable with silence—we allow the words that have been shared to be in the space but not to so dominate the space that we cannot at the same time be attentive to the witness of the Spirit.

THE DIRECTEE'S RESPONSE TO THE DIRECTOR

It is imperative that the directee also learns to listen well. Spiritual directors are not going to preach sermons or lead Bible studies. They are not going to share treatises on the work of the Spirit or provide insights into the character of good work or good relationships. A director might recommend a book on a pertinent subject if we sense that on prayer, marriage, work or whatever topic is at hand some good reading and learning might be helpful. But this is not a preaching or teaching session. And so the words that the director offers may well be spoken sparingly. Often we will not repeat something we have said unless asked to repeat or clarify what was meant when we spoke by way of observation.

Ask for clarification, certainly. And perhaps, with a suggestion or observation made, you might demur and wonder if the words of the director are indeed the required wisdom for this time. Spiritual directors are not infallible; we might miss the mark. But as a rule, if you are going for direction you listen to what is offered and you receive it "in Christ." And even if at first it seems hard or you cannot see the relevance of the comment or observation, the ministry of spiritual direction requires that you take oh-so-seriously what has been spoken and offered in this sacred space. So at the very least write it down and indicate that you will prayerfully consider, in the days to come, the potential significance of what has been said.

I have suggested that prior to the hour of spiritual direction, it is good to spend time writing out your impressions, thoughts and observations—those things you are bringing to share with the spiritual director. Writing thoughts and impressions down is also invaluable *after* the hour of direction. Following the meeting with the director, find quiet time, perhaps right away, to write down what you have heard from the spiritual director.

And use this brief exercise of writing to reflect on what was said. If you keep a journal, record all of this in the journal—including what at first you think might not be pertinent, including that which you perhaps did not agree with.

Then review these notes—both those that you took into your spiritual direction meeting, and those that you set down afterward when you are preparing for your next meeting with the director. Writing provides a benchmark, a way to monitor what is happening in our lives and in our prayers, to take account and be encouraged by real growth and spiritual development.

The writing exercise also helps one remember some things that the director offered that maybe did not register at the time or that did not seem immediately relevant, but which over time come to have greater significance.

While some may read all of this as rather too formal and not sufficiently personal or spontaneous, consider that in worship we need a liturgy—the order of our prayers and worship, with songs, readings, sermon and sacrament—with an appreciation that our response to the Spirit needs a form. Similarly the ministry of spiritual direction will be most fruitful if we are focused and intentional, with an order, a liturgy one might say, that provides us a way to open up a grace-filled space for our conversation. Just as in a dance there is power when both participants know the steps, there is freedom in the conversation when there is a mutual understanding of the "steps," the order or liturgy by which we will enter intentionally into conversation about that for which we have met.

The spiritual director strives to create an open and honest space—a safe space for a soul that is on a journey to the *shalom* of God. And as you come for direction, having a clear format or structure or order to the conversation frees us to then give attention to what you bring to the conversation. The intent and prayer, of course, is that this would be a venue or setting where you are true to self, honest about your experiences, freed from pretense and the need to impress. Most of all, the order in the conversation frees us to be attentive to the most important matter at hand—the presence and work of the Spirit.

6

Pastoral Ministry, Evangelism and Friendship

❧

While the focus of this book is *formal* spiritual direction—an hour of spiritual conversation with a spiritual director—it is also appropriate to consider the ways in which the classic principles and practice of spiritual direction can fruitfully inform pastoral ministry, evangelism and spiritual friendship.

PASTORAL MINISTRY

Eugene Peterson has made the observation that ancient and historical approaches to pastoral ministry recognized that this work, the ministry of spiritual direction, is integral to what it means to be a pastor. What was once central to the work of a pastor is now peripheral, and Peterson stresses that we need to find a way to get it back to the center—recovering this simple yet profound and relevant work of providing others with a ministry of co-discernment, "teaching people to pray, helping parishioners discern the presence of grace in events and feelings, affirming the presence of God at the very heart of life," all from the perspective of a biblical spirituality instead of, as he puts it, the "merely psychological or sociological."[1]

It is a cardinal principle of pastoral ministry that the defining relationship and connection for the Christian is not, ultimately, with the pastor and the church but with the Lord. Indeed, one of the deep commitments of each pastor should be that a parishioner grows increasingly in her or his own capacity to know God, respond to the call of Christ on her or his life and walk in the Spirit, the very Spirit that dwells in each one.

Thus, in leading worship, in preaching and in pastoral leadership and care, the perspective of spiritual direction frees us from needing to control, or in any way presuming to know how God is at work in the life of another. Rather, we are always fostering, from every angle, the way in which each person can take personal responsibility for their own faith journey. So our comments and observations as pastors are always offered from this perspective and vision: we are co-discerners, companions on the way. In other words, spiritual direction may be one aspect of a pastor's ministry but actually also deeply influences *each* dimension of pastoral work—the way we approach biblical texts and preach these texts, the kinds of conversations we have in the foyer, the way that we give leadership to administrative concerns and committee meetings.

It may be a very brief conversation after morning worship; it could be a side conversation over a lunch meeting to discuss a business concern of the church. As pastors, we know there are many moments and times, in the midst of our many conversations and meetings, to offer a word here or there, in a brief but nevertheless sacred moment and space to recognize that we are in a position to speak of how God may be present to this situation and to this concern or issue that this person or this group is facing. In every conversation, we attend to the presence of Christ, who is always the third party in our midst.

Keep in mind, however, that pastors and other religious leaders love to teach. We are trained to understand theology and explain doctrine and Scripture. But in spiritual direction, we set aside this proclivity and we learn to listen and ask, with the directee, what it is that God is communicating to their heart and mind. This is not to discount teaching or the importance of theological and biblical instruction; it is merely to emphasize that spiritual direction is the essential *complement* to teaching and should not be co-opted by teaching. A director may conclude that this person needs more basic teaching; it is merely that this is not the time or the place for that to happen.

Spiritual direction is an essential counterpoint to the work of teaching and preaching. We are in conversation, as pastors, with others knowing that God is present to them and that the wealth of our spiritual heritage is available to them to help them discern and makes sense of the work of God in their lives. And yet, the demands on the pastoral ministry seem hell-bent on discouraging this kind of attentiveness—in our own lives, first, but then in conversation with others, as we attend to them and discern with them the manifold and diverse ways in which grace might be present to them.

Making spiritual direction an integral dimension of pastoral ministry requires two things. First, we need to slow down. While we cannot be all things to all people all the time, we can pace our lives and our work so that conversations are not rushed, and so we are truly present to another in these conversations. Second, we need to learn how to be attentive to the presence and work of the Spirit, meaning that we do not default to viewing people through pragmatic or psychological lenses. Not pragmatic, in that we are only thinking of whether a person is useful to us, and not psychological, in that our primary agenda is an analysis, trying to figure out if this person is emotionally needy or unfulfilled. Rather, our orientation is that we view the other as a fellow pilgrim who God has brought into our path for conversation, and this encounter requires attentiveness to the presence of God in our lives.

EVANGELISM

We can speak of spiritual direction as a ministry that, like other ministries, has a simple goal: to help Christians live out their baptismal identity—seeking to live consistently in the grace that they have been united with Christ in his death and resurrection. And so we would naturally assume that spiritual direction is a ministry for Christian believers, one of many ministries of the Christian community that fosters spiritual growth and discipleship.

But what of those who are on the journey to faith in Christ— perhaps not yet confessing Christians? Indeed, there is also a growing appreciation of the potential of a close interplay between evangelism and spiritual direction. Typically evangelism has been thought of as a programmed approach to one who does not yet have a personal relationship with Christ. And the assumption typically has been simple: this person does not know God and if they are going to know God they need to know certain things, believe certain things and agree to live in the light of these truths. With this goes the assumption that this individual does not know God or have a relationship with God until they believe these things to be true—typically truths about the person of Christ and the work of Christ on the cross. Evangelism is then thought to be that ministry that speaks of these truths about Christ Jesus that must be affirmed followed by a call to accept these truths.

But consider another perspective. Could it be that God is actually at work in the life of each person? Everyone? And that evangelism is not so much a preprogrammed series of questions or principles to be shared, as a particular response to this person, at this stage of life, in response to how God is already present to and at work in this person?

God is calling each person to himself. It is not that God is in heaven and waiting for us to believe in him before granting us his salvation. In other words, it is not that God is passive, ready and willing to reach out to us, but doing nothing until we believe or accept God into our lives. Rather, *God is calling* and by the Spirit drawing each person to himself through Christ. God does not wait; God initiates. God calls. And this call is always specific and particular: God is calling *this* person to himself, and that call is deeply conditioned by the situation in which this person lives and the circumstances of their life and their particular points of openness to the work of the Spirit.

Further, however firm a person may be that he or she is an atheist, God never leaves himself without a witness to his love and presence. A conversion or a response to God will consistently be a response to the particular demonstration of God's love to this person—however much this person may have rejected God in the past.

Conversion is an act of response to the initiative of God and to the grace of God. We can say "God so loved the world," but the genius of evangelism may well be that we foster and encourage this person, who is a potential follower of Christ, to see how this love is evident in their own life, how God has been gracious and merciful, and how God has and is drawing this person to Christ.

Evangelism always considers how God is at work in this person's life at this time. Does this mean that there is no place for group proclamation of the gospel? Am I suggesting there is no place for preaching, and evangelistic preaching in particular? Not at all! Rather, what I am pressing for is an appreciation that evangelism is not merely proclamation, but also attentive listening to how God is present to the ididual.

And the evangelist, as spiritual director, can never make assumptions. Indeed, the heart of the matter is that the person who is on the journey to faith would be the very one who recognizes the presence and call of God. We cannot assume to know how God is present to them and calling them and inviting them to come into a relationship with Christ. As with all spiritual direction, we merely come alongside and let God do the inviting, let God do the speaking and trust God to do God's work in God's time.

In other words, as an evangelist it might be very clear to us that God is calling this person, and yet, we cannot speak too soon or presume to know the voice of God. Further, it must be stressed that a person comes to faith in Christ in the timing of God. We may wish to keep a log of all the people we have led to Christ, but the principles of spiritual direction urge us to remember that we do not control the timing of God's work in the life of another. We plant seeds; we water seeds. But only God gives the harvest in the life of another person. God does God's work in the timing of God.

For many years, I have been reading and studying conversion narratives. While it is not obvious in each conversion, I am struck by the frequency with which these narratives often include reference to a significant companion along the way who so often plays a pivotal part in the work of God in bringing a person to faith in Christ. And what impresses me is that the part played does not come close to fitting our stereotype of the Christian evangelist.

I am thinking, for example, of the role of Simplician in St. Augustine's journey to faith. Simplician succeeded Ambrose as bishop of Milan in the fourth century, serving only three or four years before his death. But surely his most significant impact was as spiritual father to many, including Augustine, to whom he was present throughout the critical months leading up to Augustine's baptism by Ambrose. A student of Scripture, he commended the reading of the Scriptures to Augustine, confident, it seems, in the power of the Spirit through the Word to bring Augustine to faith in Christ. Indeed, the critical moment for Augustine came as he was reading Romans 13—a reading that had been commended to him by Simplician.

Or, in the journey to faith of Simone Weil, a key role was played by the priest she met in Marseilles. Weil, a brilliant young mathematician and philosopher, was forced to leave France in the late 1930s. But before embarking for New York, she and her family were in Marseilles for several weeks, and she met a Dominican priest, Father J. M. Perrin. As she put it in her autobiographical reflections, she was trying to decide if she would become a Catholic. So much had happened in her tortured life—so many impulses that prompted her to finally turn to and accept the love of Christ. But she was still trying to make sense of the doctrines of the church—the Trinity, the incarnation, cross and resurrection. And her conversations with Father Perrin finally led to her acceptance of these ancient mysteries of the faith.

Then also, I think of Dorothy Day. Her entire being longed to be an advocate for the poor and for the laboring class, particularly those who lived and worked in the lower east side of New York. And as a young Marxist/socialist in the 1920s, she was just not convinced that the church cared for the poor. So much attracted her to the Christian faith, and there was a side of her that knew the Marxist ideology could not satisfy the deep yearnings of her heart. And yet, her baseline was a deep concern for the poor. It is so significant that after a series of personal crises, she came to Staten Island and there, while in personal turmoil, she met an extraordinary nun, Sister Aloysia of the local Sisters of Charity, with whom she developed a friendship. Beautifully portrayed in the film about Dorothy Day, *Entertaining Angels*, Sister Aloysia demonstrated to Dorothy a mature Christian believer who was caring for the poor. And as Dorothy came increasingly to see her need for God, she did so while working for the poor side by side with this nun who patiently accepted Dorothy and the slow journey that Dorothy was making toward faith in Christ.

While none of these three were spiritual directors by definition, in a very profound sense they were. They understood something at the heart of direction and they were present to someone who was on the way to faith. And there is much here that is instructive. A spiritual director knows that we are called to trust God with the lives of others—and thus with this relationship and this potential convert to faith in Christ. This requires both sensitivity and patience. We let God do God's work in God's time. And rarely will one individual play a definitive role in a person's coming to faith. When we ask "Who led this person to Christ?" the typical answer will be: the Spirit, the Holy Spirit, used various ways and means, people here and there, to listen and to speak and to be a means by which a person came to faith.

This means that in conversation with a potential follower of Jesus, we can listen to their story and, as appropriate, we can also ask: So where is God in this? Where do *you* sense God is present in your life? Do you have a sense of the love and goodness of God? If so, how is God demonstrating his call on your life? Rather than assuming or imposing what we think must surely be God's agenda, we ask the other, the potential convert to Christ, to discern the presence of God and the actions and initiative of God.

Something must be stressed here: conversion is not ultimately about believing certain things to be true. Rather, conversion and transformation ultimately come as this person, in their time, meets Christ. In real time. Or better, it comes as Christ reveals himself, personally, to this person. This is the transforming encounter. And Christ will reveal himself in his own time.

Yes, of course, teaching is essential. And yes, certainly, we must affirm the vital place of preaching—the proclamation of the gospel and the faithful exposition of the Scriptures. This is basic and foundational. But then, alongside the proclaimed word, there is spiritual direction and personal conversations that accompany the preaching, as we encourage this person to hear, on their own terms, the call of Christ, to sense his presence and love and, in time, to respond to the offer of his grace.

We typically think of evangelism as speaking the gospel. Evangelists, we think, are talkers and preachers. But from the vantage point of spiritual direction, an evangelist is first and foremost a good listener. While we surely speak, we cannot speak well until we listen well. Further, we are comfortable with God's work and God's timing. So we can learn to wait and be patient. And let God do God's work in God's time.

FRIENDSHIP

In so many ways the principles and practices of spiritual direction are relevant to our commitment to be a good friend. One of the greatest gifts of God to us is the gift of friends. We may actually have relatively few—many will perhaps only have two or three or four friends—who are dearer to us than family, soul mates in the journey of life and faith. These friendships are formed over time; they are the fruit of extended conversations and shared experiences. The older we get the more we come to appreciate that in our senior years the most precious gifts we have are these—the friends we have made, or better, the friends that God has given us along the way.

Though friends are a gift from God, this kind of friendship is the fruit of intentionality—notably, intentional conversation, especially conversation that takes us beyond the topics we commonly talk about: our work and our daily activities. Further, in conversation with a friend we have opportunity to speak about our convictions, our passions and our interior life. We have a safe space to speak about joy and sorrow, fear and discouragement, anger and disappointment. While there are many elements to a conversation between friends, there are three threads that can draw on the ancient practice of spiritual direction.

First, if indeed it is the case that the footprints or traces of the Spirit's presence are felt, specifically in the emotional contours of our hearts and minds, then it is essential that we foster our capacity to speak truthfully and with freedom about what is emerging in our hearts, that is, what is happening to us emotionally.

I think of that rich chapter in my life where in meeting regularly with a friend we only had one agenda item: to reflect together on each other's joys and sorrows. "What has brought you joy?" and "Where has there been sorrow?" we would ask each other. And implied in this conversation we considered: where is God in this, and where do we sense God is leading and guiding and encouraging?

For this to be done well requires that we move beyond pretense, beyond facades, beyond the need to impress. With a friend we are free to speak of our fears and our feelings of discouragement and even of anger. If not with a friend, then where? Many people—though in my experience this is more so the case with men—never really have deep friends and they never truly speak of what they are feeling. And the two go together: to have a friend is to speak of matters of the heart. It is to have a safe space to speak, to think carefully about what we are experiencing and to have another to share our joy—which deepens that joy—and to share and bear with us our sorrows—which softens the blow, the pain, the depth of the sorrow.

Second, a spiritual friend is also one who comes alongside in times of choice. Much like a spiritual director—perhaps in complement to the work of a spiritual director in our lives—a spiritual friend can be an invaluable companion when we are faced with a critical decision.

I must stress: the choice is ours—if we are to marry, if we are to accept a job assignment, and so on. The choice is ours to make, and it is not true friendship when we impose on our friends the expectation that they will choose for us. They have enough complications in their lives already, no doubt.

But it is a profound gift to have a friend listen in, so to speak, on our decision-making process. To challenge us and encourage us and gently call us to account when we are perhaps ignoring a significant factor, when we are choosing for all the wrong reasons, when we are rushing into a decision or, of course, when we are simply procrastinating. A true friend will encourage us without flattery, but more, a true friend will also tell us what they see and hear without fear of hurting us because we know that it is love that binds us together. They will tell us the truth: no sentimentality, no making it easy for us but rather helping us see reality so that we can navigate that reality with courage and grace.

The reference to courage brings up the third crucial aspect of our spiritual conversation between friends: mutual encouragement. As friends, we are always attentive to the need for apt words in season, words of affirmation (again, without flattery), words of insight, words of hope. Our friends encourage us. In a deeply fragmented and broken world, we have so much that sets us back, and throws us off our game and unsettles us. And the value of a true friendship is surely this: we always go our separate ways once more encouraged—knowing again that God is God and that God holds all things together.

So, while we speak of the formal relationship of spiritual direction in these pages, we also want to keep in mind the idea that the principles and practices of spiritual direction can be integrated into other dimensions of our lives and ministries, including our friendships.

7

The Qualities and Character of a Director

If, as you read, you find yourself feeling that this is precisely what you would like to have — someone to walk alongside as companion and guide, directing you to the work of the Spirit in your life — then what's next? Well, we may first need a good dose of realism. John of the Cross made the observation that good directors are few. Indeed, that was no more or less true of sixteenth-century Spain than it is in our times and in our cities. And so finding a director may take some persistence. I am reminded of the hermit desert monks, living in caves, far from the cities, far from any social interaction. Sincere pilgrims headed to the desert to secure their counsel and spiritual wisdom. And they had to be patient and persistent, often walking many days only to find that the wise saint who they sought had moved farther into the desert to avoid the crowds. And there was no way to book an appointment online. One had to follow farther into the desert and perhaps find that this wise person was not all that congenial, but might wait for hours

in silence before he finally agreed to listen to the pilgrim who
had traveled for so many days.

Or I think of Elisha, the prophet who was junior to Elijah
his mentor. Elisha actively sought the blessing of Elijah and
would not let him go until he knew that his own ministry would
be marked by the anointing that had already been given through
Elijah. Elisha took the initiative and sought out the blessing of
the older man. In like manner, it may well be that a spiritual
director may not just show up at our door. It may require some
attentiveness and discernment, some persistence and resolve.

Some of us may find individuals who know about spiritual
direction and perhaps are trained as directors. But it is important to also note that there is likely much spiritual wisdom
close at hand, within the church community of which you
are a part.

I think back to an older man, the age of my father, who I met
with with regularly over many years long before I had ever heard
of spiritual direction. In retrospect, I came to see that he was a
wise and able "director" even though we did not use this kind of
language; he was simply being a wise pastor and spiritual elder
and friend to a younger man. And his presence in my life, as I
look back on those years, was a tremendous gift from God. We
met regularly, every few weeks, over the course of several years.

And so perhaps we should not insist too much on seeking a
"spiritual director" but simply consider: is there an older man
or an older woman with whom I could meet regularly for spiritual counsel and friendship?

FIVE ESSENTIAL CHARACTERISTICS

What do we look for in a spiritual director, or simply an elder
companion on the road? I have identified five essential qual-

ities or characteristics that, it seems to me, are indispensable for one to play this role or ministry in the life of another.

1. Effective spiritual direction requires a basic understanding of the theology of the Christian life—particularly the theology of the Spirit. While formal theological training is not essential, one can hardly expect to be attentive to the Spirit without a biblically informed theological understanding of the way of the Spirit. Of course, there is more to the theological foundations of spiritual direction than the theology of the Spirit, as I noted in chapter two, but a nuanced understanding of the ways and work of the Spirit—or pneumatology—seems to be a basic requirement.

2. Most effective spiritual directors are those who have some awareness of the history of Christian spirituality so that they can draw on the wisdom or heritage of the church in their spiritual counsel. Perhaps one spiritual director is able to draw on the wisdom of the church fathers; or another has been immersed in the writings of Catherine of Sienna, Julian of Norwich or Teresa of Ávila; or another provides spiritual direction with a profound awareness of John Calvin's theology of the Spirit and of the spiritual life. Others will no doubt draw on the wisdom of more contemporary writers—Dietrich Bonhoeffer or Henri Nouwen or Eugene Peterson, for example.

But the main point is that they are able to draw on wisdom from the spiritual heritage of the church. This is important for several reasons, but for one in particular: a great danger in spiritual direction is that we presume and impose—presume that our experience, our personal experience, is the norm, and then we impose this expectation on the one whom for whom we provide spiritual counsel. Reading the spiritual masters helps to put our own experience in perspective.

A person who knows something of the spiritual masters can draw on that wisdom as they help us make sense of our experience. Beware of those who suggest that they know the Bible and that is all they need to know! A director certainly needs to be biblically literate. Wise directors and spiritual guides *are* able to draw on the wisdom of the Scriptures as they listen and respond to what is being offered in the conversation. Yet what I am suggesting here is that the Spirit has continued to guide and teach the church throughout the centuries (Jn 16:12-15), and that wise spiritual directors are those who have learned from the spiritual masters in the history of the church. And more, they are able to enter into this ministry of spiritual direction with a vision for the spiritual life that has been informed and shaped by this spiritual heritage.

3. Compassion is surely a key characteristic of a spiritual director. We so deeply need another who is not so much a judge and critic—we have plenty of those!—but who comes to us with empathetic attentiveness to the human predicament. By this I do not mean someone who either sentimentalizes our situation or is soft on the destructive power of sin. Not for a moment. Rather, even as Christ was able to sympathize with our human predicament (Heb 4:14-16), so a spiritual director brings this kind of compassionate priestly presence into our lives.

A spiritual director is not a critic. Directors will rarely use the word *should* in their conversation—perhaps not at all. The deep energy that sustains our engagement in conversation, and that animates this conversation, is a shared awareness that, in the wonderful phrase that arises so often in the writing of Charles Williams, we are all "under the mercy." An exchange with a spiritual director is an "under-the-mercy conversation."

And it is surely the director who sets the tone—both in the offer of compassion and in the regular reminder to the directee to be self-compassionate.

4. Next is the capacity for double listening. A good spiritual director is one who is a listener—one who knows how to be fully present to another. And yet the genius of their listening is that they listen—still attentive to the directee, but at one and the same time, not as a distraction, but as a vital counterpoint—to the presence of Christ in the room, in this space, in this conversation.

Now it must be stressed: double listening does not mean that we prioritize the voice of God over that of the directee, meaning that we ignore what we are hearing from the directee. We are here to listen to *this* child of God. What I mean is that we listen to God by listening to this person's account of their faith and the challenges of their faith journey.

5. Finally, there must be confidentiality of a sort that a spiritual director gets it, deep in their way of being, that the content of a conversation for spiritual direction is a sacred, private space.

As in friendship, nothing is so insidious to true relationship and community as gossip. And in spiritual direction, the sacredness of the time and space is fundamental and essential. I sometimes jokingly say with a Roman Catholic priest as your director, you know that what you have shared is completely and utterly safe—sacred and confidential. But if you share with an evangelical pastor, watch it—your story, with the name no doubt changed, will show up as a sermon illustration in two or three weeks (these preachers are so desperate for illustrations!).

This is certainly an unfair characterization. But the point is made: we can only truly and wisely offer direction if we understand the absolute need for confidentiality. Are their exceptions? Certainly. If there is the capacity that this person might hurt themselves or another, or if they have committed a crime and by law we must report it—perhaps the abuse of children. But as a rule this is a sacred and confidential space.

Of course, the fundamental quality of a director is that she or he is a person of prayer, and further, someone whose quality of life and prayer is one from which we would like to learn. Often, a spiritual director is in a very different field or sphere of work; but there is a quality of life—equanimity, intensity, joy and personal focus, perhaps—that leads us to think that this is the person with whom we would like to reflect on our own spiritual journey.

TRAINING AND GENDER

Should a spiritual director have formal training? Some training is certainly appropriate, but as a rule, the best training is to be directed by a qualified director and learned from the experience of receiving direction. There are some basic skills and capacities, and while formal training might be appropriate, there are many mature Christians who are more than capable of being companions along the way.

Should a spiritual director have some kind of clear line of accountability for this ministry? This would certainly be an ideal, in that these kinds of conversations are so open to manipulation and abuse. In most cases, the spiritual director is likely part of a religious order, or is an ordained minister within a Protestant denomination, or is a faculty member of a theological school. Each of these provides some measure of institutional or juridical accountability. A spiritual director should be able to answer the question: who am I accountable to for the quality of pastoral care that I offer through this ministry of spiritual direction?

A qualified director also recognizes the limits of direction. At times, potential directees really need some good theological and biblical study before they can take full advantage of this ministry. They need a theological orientation to the work of the Spirit. And in other cases, they are wrestling with emotional or relational challenges that really need the expertise of a trained counselor. If a person is wrestling with depression, for example, it is wise for the director to either ask that the person first see a counselor or, at the very least, only offer direction if at the same time the directee is seeing a counselor to address the depression. Only then would the spiritual direction be worthwhile.

Should spiritual direction be gender specific—with men serving as directors to men and women to women? While we do not need to be hard and fast on this one, as a general rule I would suspect that it is most fruitful for men to be meeting with men and women with women.

TRANSITIONS

Not every director is suitable for every directee. A very qualified and effective director may well not be suitable for a given person at a particular point in his or her life. It is not a problem, then, for either the director or the directee to choose, at first, to merely test the waters, and see if there is a resonance, a connection, that can make this relationship fruitful. And perhaps after meeting two or three times, one or both might agree that while these times were good, they will not continue to meet. This is not a problem or a matter of failure or a reason for any embarrassment.

Spiritual directors must have strong egos, able to graciously accept that they are not the ideal director for everyone and that, ultimately, it is up to the directee to decide if they will continue to meet. Though it is also fine and appropriate for a director to simply say, "As I have thought and prayed about our relationship, I have concluded that it might be more fruitful for you to meet with someone else for direction." Again, there is no sense of failure or shame in offering these words, but merely a recognition of the limits of direction.

I met with Father Tom Green for a number of years; he was a wonderful director. But after more than a dozen years, I had to come to the conclusion that as our friendship had grown and we had various opportunities to minister together, co-presenting and teaching together in a number of venues, it might be more fruitful for me to begin to meet with another person for direction. I concluded that no sentimentality or nostalgia or a false sense of loyalty to Father Green was going to keep me from finding the right kind of spiritual direction I needed, as I moved into a new chapter of my life. And, of course, Father Green fully understood and supported my decision. He assured me of his ongoing friendship and prayer, knowing that he could never be viewed as indispensable to my life, my work and my prayers.

8

The Qualities and Character of a Directee

Who is ready? What does it take to be able and prepared to enter into a relationship of spiritual direction and to benefit from this ministry?

On the one hand, surely all who are called into and preparing for religious leadership should have someone who serves them as a spiritual director. I am thinking of all who are in formal theological education in preparation for pastoral and religious leadership. Indeed, I would be inclined to go further and say that all pastors should have this as a vital dimension of their own ongoing formation—not merely while they are in preparation for pastoral ministry but throughout their active professional lives in leadership in the church. Pastors need at least one relationship where their pastoral facade can be set aside, where authenticity can be nurtured, where hard questions about the state of their own souls can be raised. And indeed, we never graduate from our need for direction: at every stage of life, work and ministry, there is a profound need for a companion, one who comes alongside as a co-discerner and encourager. I serve as the president of a Christian university and seminary; I consider it imperative and a vital dimension of my responsibility to those I serve that I am in spiritual direction. Pastors owe it to their congregations—indeed, if I were a lay elder of a congregation I would be forthright in expecting our pastor to be in direction.

Beyond this, many if not most laypersons would also benefit from this ministry. But then for pastors and laypersons alike, it is appropriate to recognize that while, in principle, all Christians could benefit from this ministry, some are in a greater position to take full advantage of the opportunity that may be given to them. It is really only fair: if we are going to seek direction and ask another to be a director to us, then it is appropriate to ask, What necessary perspectives, dispositions and actions should we bring to this relationship?

First, of course, the *desire* to grow in faith, hope and love is foundational—that we come to this conversation with a spiritual director as one who is eager to grow, eager to learn, willing to see ourselves in the truth and longing to be more mature in our faith journey. We come with a holy discontent—not an impatience, but a desire, a profound willingness, to be changed and to grow in grace.

And this will be evident early on. Is there a desire and commitment to diligence in prayer and spiritual practice? Is there a personal discipline and management of one's time and priorities that will make the time of spiritual direction fruitful?

Second is the need for meekness and humility. This is the same quality or disposition that we necessarily bring to an encounter with the Word, in worship. The book of James speaks of meekness as an essential disposition (Jas 1:21)—the humility of gracious acceptance of the purposes and call of God on our lives. We are open, receptive and teachable.

This meekness or humility means that we come with an open mind and heart—not gullible (we are still discerning) and not compliant (the director is not infallible), but still with a gracious vulnerability: willing and eager, with open heart and open hands, to hear what is offered to us by the spiritual director. Yes, there might be a gentle resistance if the word from the director at first seems to make no sense to us. But as a rule, we come to our time of spiritual direction with meekness—open to the words and input from our director.

And third, our approach to direction should be intentional. We come to the hour of conversation with our director having given time and attention to what we will say. Take time, slow, methodical, undistracted time, to ask: what have been the themes of my life that seem to be significant markers in my life? (See chapter three on the content of spiritual direction.) As noted, I have found it valuable to ask those who come to me for direction to prepare a one-page set of notes. It gives the director a way to be ready for the conversation and to anticipate where it might go. But without doubt, the primary benefit is for the directee: it is most vital to come into the conversation having given some careful thought to what God may be calling you to share with the spiritual director.

Then it follows that if the director makes suggestions for actions we might take coming out of the conversation, and if we take direction seriously, we take notes and we act. We implement. We are not toying at this; we owe it to the director to, in so far as we can, act on the suggestions and observations offered.

Most of all, both director and directee come to this ministry with a single agenda: to know the purposes and callings of God in the life of one person, the directee. They both desire to be present and focused enough to the way in which God's Spirit is prompting and guiding, and to cultivate the discernment to be able to both recognize the presence and footprints of the Spirit and to respond appropriately.

Now we conclude with a deeper look at the role of the Holy Spirit, the ultimate director of our souls and our lives.

9

The Holy Spirit as Spiritual Director

In the end there is really only one director of the spiritual life, and this is the Spirit of God, the third person of the Trinity. The ministry of direction comes down to this: fostering our capacity to attend to the work and movement of the Spirit in our lives.

Here is where it might be appropriate to register a concern with one recent trend in spiritual direction. Increasingly, it would seem that directors are giving focus to how an individual can take some time to get away, and come to a greater awareness of themselves and their ego needs and concerns. While there may be some profit here—indeed it could be quite a fruitful process and exercise—we should not confuse this with the ancient and essential work of spiritual direction.

The genius of direction is the presence of God, in the room, in the conversation, in the life of the directee. And true spiritual direction then is one of gently but constantly bringing us back to how God is at work in our lives. Without doubt, the best way to do this is to foster our capacity to live our lives in the light of the life, death, resurrection and ascension of Christ Jesus. This is so for a very simple reason: that this is precisely the work of the Spirit—drawing us ever more into union with Christ and fostering within us the capacity to live as followers, as disciples, of Christ. The ministry of spiritual direction is a gift that is offered to us as a means to foster our capacity to attend to the voice of Jesus. And when we put it this way, we are reminded that nothing matters more than this: to know, love and serve Jesus, to hear his voice, the voice of the Good Shepherd, and to grow in our capacity to abide in Christ even as Christ abides in us.

This is the work of the Holy Spirit.

C. S. LEWIS'S ASLAN: A PICTURE OF THE SPIRIT AT WORK IN OUR LIVES

In the Chronicles of Narnia by C. S. Lewis, one of my favorite encounters is that between the Lion, Aslan, and the boy Shasta in the third book in the series, *The Horse and His Boy*.

Shasta, though young, has lived a rather extraordinary life, with highs and lows—an orphan who did not know his parents, raised by an unkind fisherman, almost sold as a slave and then on the run across barren terrain and deserts and threatened by all kinds of evil forces, most notably by lions that seem to endanger him again and again. Along the way he befriends a talking horse and later a girl, Aravis, and her horse, Hwin. They all four make their way across the dangerous landscape, and while en-route they again encounter a lion chasing them, and in the chase the lion takes a swipe at Aravis and wounds her.

Then later in the narrative, Shasta is traveling alone through deep fog. He is lonely and feeling abandoned and hard done by. And he is hungry and has nowhere to stay. He is feeling sorry for himself. As he is walking along, slowly in the dark fog, he gradually becomes aware of a presence near at hand. And then he comes to a growing awareness that the presence is rather substantial. This presence seems benevolent, so he opens up a little and speaks out loud about the troubles of his life, still feeling sorry for himself. In particular he complains about all the lions that have caused him grief.

The presence near to him says in response, "I do not call you unfortunate." Shasta protests and insists, "Don't you think it was bad luck to meet so many lions?"

And out of the fog he hears the reply: "There was only one lion."

Shasta immediately argues, "What on earth do you mean? I've just told you there were at least two the first night, and—"

And again, still in the fog, unable to see who is speaking, Shasta gets a response: "There was only one: but he was swift of foot."

Shasta then asks the obvious question: "How do you know?"

And the voice speaks these words: "I was the lion. . . . I was the lion who forced you to join with Aravis. I was the cat who comforted you among the houses of the dead. I was the lion who drove the jackals away from you while you slept. I was the lion who gave the Horses the new strength of fear for the last mile so that you should reach King Lune in time. And I was the lion you do not remember who pushed the boat in which you lay, a child near to death, so that it came to the shore where a man sat, wakeful at midnight, to receive you."

Shasta sees all this benevolent presence and goodness, but then, no surprise, he still has a question—given that in the desert, when the horses were being chased, his companion Aravis had been wounded by the lion. And so his exchange with the lion continues:

"Then it was you who wounded Aravis?"

"It was I."

Shasta understandably asks, "But what for?" And the lion responds, "Child . . . I am telling you your story, not hers. I tell no one any story but his own."[1]

In this account of Aravis and the lion, Lewis captures the genius of spiritual direction: to come alongside and co-discern with us the presence of the lion, the presence of Aslan, the presence and work of the Spirit in our lives. We are only truly able to tell our stories when we see how each story is grace filled. It is so easy to bemoan all that seems to have gone wrong and all that seems difficult and lacking and unhelpful. The gift of spiritual direction is to help us, in the "fog" of our circumstances, to be attentive to the presence of the Other.

And more, Lewis so very rightly highlights that it was not for Shasta to know the meaning of the wound that Aravis received. That was only for Aravis to know.

Spiritual direction is personal, individual and particular. As directees, we are attentive to how God is present to our lives and are not so much concerned with Christ's agenda in the lives of others. We are discovering how God is present to us, at this time and in this place, rather than asking the director about other people. We are looking for the ways in which God is active in our lives: directing, prompting and calling. And it is the ministry of spiritual direction that fosters this very capacity.

What we learn, of course, is that the triune God—Father, Son and Spirit—is for us and not against us, that God loves us and has always loved us and has been present to us in and around our lives, even when we did not recognize this presence. And through direction, we learn to lean into this presence and to trust ever more in the goodness and providential care of God.

Notes

Chapter 1: *The Ministry of Spiritual Direction*

[1] Simon Chan, *Spiritual Theology: A Systematic Study of the Christian Life* (Downers Grove, IL: InterVarsity Press, 1998), p. 226.

[2] William A. Barry and William J. Connolly, *The Practice of Spiritual Direction* (San Francisco: Harper & Row, 1982), p. 11.

[3] In the Benedictine tradition, we naturally reference Thomas Merton, the Trappist monk from the United States; see his *Spiritual Direction and Meditation* (Wheathampstead, UK: Anthony Clarke, 1975). For the Orthodox tradition, consider John Chryssavgis, *Soul Mending: The Art of Spiritual Direction* (Brookline, MA: Holy Cross Orthodox Press, 2000). From an Anglican perspective, there are a number of valuable guides, including the last chapter in F. P. Harton, *The Elements of the Spiritual Life* (London: SPCK, 1932), and more recently Peter Ball, *Journey into Truth* (Lincoln, RI: Andrew Mowbray, 1998; also published as *Anglican Spiritual Direction*). And from the Reformed perspective, there is the classic by Richard Baxter, *The Reformed Pastor* (London, 1808).

Chapter 2: *Theological Perspectives*

[1] John of the Cross, *The Collected Works of St. John of the Cross; Living Flame of Love* (Washington, DC: ICS Publications, 1979), bk. 3, 29-67.

[2] William A. Barry, *Spiritual Direction and the Encounter with God: A Theological Inquiry* (New York: Paulist Press, 1992), p. 11.

Chapter 6: *Pastoral Ministry, Evangelism and Friendship*

[1] Eugene H. Peterson, *Working the Angles: The Shape of Pastoral Integrity* (Grand Rapids: Eerdmans, 1987), p. 104.

Chapter 9: *The Holy Spirit as Spiritual Director*

[1] C. S. Lewis, *The Horse and His Boy* (London: Fontana Lions, 1954), pp. 129-30.

For Further Reading

Barry, William A. *Spiritual Direction and the Encounter with God: A Theological Inquiry*. New York: Paulist Press, 1992.

Barry, William A., and William J. Connolly. *The Practice of Spiritual Direction*. San Francisco: Harper & Row, 1982.

Chan, Simon. *Spiritual Theology: A Systematic Study of the Christian Life*. Downers Grove, IL: InterVarsity Press, 1998 (see especially chapter 12).

Dunne, Tad. *Spiritual Mentoring: Guiding People Through Spiritual Exercises to Life Decisions*. San Francisco: HarperSanFrancisco, 1991.

English, John. *Spiritual Freedom: From an Experience of the Ignatian Exercises to the Art of Spiritual Guidance*, 2nd edition. Chicago: Loyola Press, 1995.

Green, Thomas H. *The Friend of the Bridegroom: Spiritual Direction and the Encounter with Christ*. Notre Dame, IN: Ave Maria, 2000.

John of the Cross. *The Collected Works of St. John of the Cross; Living Flame of Love*. Translated by Kieran Kavanaugh and Otilio Rodriguez. Washington, DC: ICS Publications, 1979 (see especially Book 3, #29-67).

Merton, Thomas. *Spiritual Direction and Meditation*. Wheathampstead, UK: Anthony Clarke, 1975.

Peterson, Eugene. *Working the Angles: The Shape of Pastoral Integrity*. Grand Rapids: Eerdmans, 1987 (see especially pp. 103-30).

Puhl, Louis J. *The Spiritual Exercises of St. Ignatius*. Allahabad: St. Paul Publications, 1975.

Smith, Gordon T. *Alone with the Lord: A Guide to a Day of Prayer*. Vancouver: Regent College, 2003.

Smith, Gordon T. *Courage and Calling: Maximizing Your God-given Potential*, 2nd ed. Downers Grove, IL: InterVarsity Press, 2010.

Smith, Gordon T. *The Voice of Jesus: Discernment, Prayer and the Witness of the Spirit*. Downers Grove, IL: InterVarsity Press, 2001.

** formatio**
TRADITION. EXPERIENCE.
TRANSFORMATION.

Formatio books from InterVarsity Press follow the rich tradition of the church in the journey of spiritual formation. These books are not merely about being informed, but about being transformed by Christ and conformed to his image. Formatio stands in InterVarsity Press's evangelical publishing tradition by integrating God's Word with spiritual practice and by prompting readers to move from inward change to outward witness. InterVarsity Press uses the chambered nautilus for Formatio, a symbol of spiritual formation because of its continual spiral journey outward as it moves from its center. We believe that each of us is made with a deep desire to be in God's presence. Formatio books help us to fulfill our deepest desires and to become our true selves in light of God's grace.

BOOKS BY GORDON T. SMITH

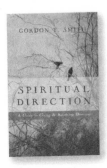

Spiritual Direction

Listening to God in
Times of Choice

Beginning Well

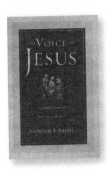

The Voice of Jesus

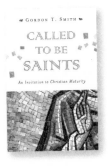

Called to Be Saints

Courage and Calling